C000104247

the butterflies and the burnings

Also by Anne Blonstein

sand.soda.lime, Broken Boulder Press, 2002

the blue pearl, Salt Publishing, 2003

worked on screen, Poetry Salzburg, 2005

from eternity to personal pronoun, Gribble Press, 2005

that those lips had language, Plan B Press, 2005

thou shalt not kill, dusie wee chaps, 2007

hairpin loop, Bright Hill Press, 2007

memory's morning, Shearsman Books, 2008

correspondence with nobody, ellectrique press, 2008

First printing, Anne Blonstein 2009

Non-commercial reproduction of this work is permitted and encouraged. Reproduction for profit is prohibited except by permission of the author.

ISBN 978-0-6151-8579-8

the butterflies and the burnings

anne blonstein

acknowledgements

Poems in this collection first appeared, sometimes in slightly different versions, in *Collages & Bricolages, Colorado Review, Mesechabe, New Orleans Review, The European Legacy, New Trends in Feminine Spirituality: The Holy Women of Liège and their Impact, So to Speak, Tessera,* and *Weber Studies.* The author would like to thank the editors of these publications.

A grant from Canton Baselland in 1997 to support the writing of some of the pieces in this collection is gratefully acknowledged.

Dusie Press
: Zürich, Switzerland : editor@dusie.org : http://www.dusie.org :

contents

euphrosyne: the donning of a scheme

There appears to be no evidence that this Euphrosyne ever existed.

powerfully an unfading moment proposes brilliantly green labials their privitate leaves styled in doubt spotted with open and within their fastidiously dyed sight prior to deliberated labels the plot embraces.

paphuncius of alexandria although married for many years remained childless until, after appealing for the prayers of the abbot and monks of a convent he visited frequently, he finally became the proud parent of a child. baptized at the age of seven, at twelve euphrosyne lost her mother. some years later, from many suitors, her father selected the richest and most noble and then took euphrosyne to the monastery and with munificent gifts begged for her the blessing and prayers of the abbot. they stayed there three days, during which time euphrosyne much admired the holy life of the monks. shortly thereafter, on the anniversary of his election, the abbot had a feast prepared to which he invited all his friends. he sent a monk to the house of paphuncius to request his presence at this entertainment. but her father was not at home, giving euphrosyne the opportunity for a long conversation with the monk whom she questioned intensely about monastic life, expressing fears for her soul should she remain in the secular world. whereupon the monk urged her to a disguise and, while paphuncius partook of the abbot's festival, to enter a monastery. this she did, taking the name smaridanus, or smaragdus, the emerald. but the beauty of his face so distracted the monks from their devotions, they thought he was a devil come to tempt them, and the abbot ordered him to remain in his cell, to say his prayers alone, and not to enter the church. with great sorrow paphuncius sought euphrosyne in all the nunneries and every other place that could possibly conceal her. at last he came for consolation to the monk, smaragdus, who comforted him, assuring him that god was taking care of euphrosyne in some good place. he continued to visit him, receiving much solace and advice for thirty-three years. after much privation and self-discipline, at the point of death, he told him who she was, beseeching him to keep her secret even after his death. but agapito, or agape, who took care of him, hearing the lamentations over him, understood who she was and told the abbot.

Baillet doubts the story, but Rosweide, the Bollandist, thinks it genuine.

angela: a folly of origins

from the beginning until the end i
scarcely wrote anything except temptations
laughing their unusual laws. espousing
by carelessly jotting down brief notes.
excessive tears of buffered milk licked through
damages of purposeful incaution.

these infestations on a small scrap of paper
support the tribulation of smothered ulcers.

i put away what little of him when he died
suddenly although she would later confirm
that what i had written quarantined
ambiguity. and dribbling at
the conclusion of the words you speak
we will continue to kiss the fibrillating
evenings. industrially betray the sex
i still have not corrected in the paper-skinned
rhythms of love. to me not only were her
previous remarks fragmentary and
lesioned i fell into a septic disease
of disturbances anticipating
intrusions. the way to completeness
tapestried the spiritless with october
afternoons. having leached the other things
about which i was inquiring were also
incomplete questions flagellated by
neglect. having paid that the following is
written to decimate complacency.

i will inform you of these unused events

which may coalesce by means of all the ways
by which i knew she was pursued.
i abscessed into duplications
after i had forced her to begin talking
alternative renunciations.
i tell the spectators i announce
the offering of the one telling me
of terrible quenchings.
i spent the summer in a torpor
of cognitive illnesses wrote these
divine words in the burning quadratics
of officialese.
i will vomit the quintessential answers
erratically and systematically
to add nothing of my own.
i junket on sexist demolitions
as the falling vulture prepares to meet
the window-sill.
i freeze in the refurnished partitions
of the first person acquiring more.
i composed my passionate pantry
with the high octane of ordinary days
when i wrote seated near to her.
i will flute the years an octave higher
than orderly and reason
why i began to write is

i

always desiring and despairing
of a tenacious lucidity.

but they divorce themselves from me saying i speak
with a quinsy and that the writing is quite
obscure because the words you read to me do
not convey the intended meaning. nor one
solution since i do not really believe
in her gliding across his boundaried

successions. in the event that fraternal
divides our familiarity. we need
occult codes for what is inconsequential
and meaningless you have written nothing to
rupture in a marvellous. our sullenness
swims through natural nouns and then she responded
to me. proving to me the deciduous
result circulates through our mouths' inceptions.
and so at that point i quit writing

syncletica: from the desert to the living

anna syncletica said: "strengthened by sleep you wake each sweet morning to a moment that offers you entry into language — that privileged apparition. perhaps you will turn a page of the kind that makes you doubt that place is an open space. here the silence burns me. fastidiously turns my body into an orifice that opens layer by layer into a plain of enclosure."

and anna syncletica spoke: "you enter these vast potholes of air seeking drinking water for the mind. but the present evades you like laughter free falling over the edge of description. not now but a passage cut off by nostalgia. the substance at the centre of an old clarity infers the plot growing cold as the smoke disposes."

and when the potential syncletica was asked if destiny joins opportunity to the expression she replied: "lately i have preferred the vision of citrus leaves from a species of uncertainty falling on a site sincerely traditional and hazardous. in the smallest matter like a grain of sand you can watch the primal film of interrogation projected on the screen of comprehension."

anna syncletica said: "a vigorous fear of the instant will affirm an exile in her labyrinth of priestly approaches. in the pageant of your gender may possibly peel and unseal the inside from the outside for a gap no more substantial than a dash through memory in tense schemes and abbreviations."

again she said: "with the power of lightning every occasion holds out for you the enigmas of never lacking in liability. like the bridal party ghosts who force you into the cave of unbarred darkness. force you to intuit pain in the embrace by measuring the angle between corpses and the principles of occidental opacity."

gudula: the slender crux

a trembling returns. that deliquescence again.
always monstrous fragments — laughing at the terseness.
another figment to compare with high serenity:
these spaces   with nocturnal illuminations.

old ideas in a prodigal patience appears
in the mist the will-o'-the-wisps dance
leftwards: but love and death could choose
different motorways. and the white flower might survive

this winter. a romance then whose leading angels
perspire. rose with a grey heart. insubstantial goods.
another version that sprang up in one morning.

poplar leaves — fall! and nourish our earth.
but as miscellaneous signs of celibate aid
you may hang in the air for at least an hour

yvette: the old estate of not turning away

the shrouds have travelled through the layers of contagion. alter the texture of skin. press the humblest against the luxurious glimmer of anaesthesia. all are tender. all ulcerates committed to the wounds that go unfelt and unnoticed. of the mouth. of the inflammatory texts where we meet the achievements. the combination of signs: "the eyes water." "the nostrils are stuffed up." "the gums putrefy." so symptoms correspond with the symbols seen. that she will come back embracing a whole series of pathological states. taking control of the thirsty book labelled woman does not claim to have put together an original collection. sullied and so forth from writer to writer. unobserving the observable. in the presence of a reality unfamiliar in terms which fail. a body covered with full stops. summoned by the paralysed side. dallying with the rotten. gentle on varicose particulars and open to infected matter. signs. appointments with amorphous differences.

properly struck by a situation and a formality. certainly watched by all the harshness of official orders. (they were led to the cemetery and buried alive.) starving reminders of hopelessness. the transient endured. lent perfumed water. the blood of a turtle. or of an infant. a question of leaving the laughter for a world that stands solemner. for a community of vast intervals scarred by scarcity. a fast asylum for the transient exiled and confined. veins punctured. waiting to belong to severance. to laws opened wide the pressure rising in transition units. mutilated evidence shifts time breathes and abides in spite of an infectious warning. sickness in the whole delight of comprehension. confident in despair delinquent at the litigated limits of no.

not a smooth line but a risk meeting the subdued the separated the wasted. individually each wish chills. in the chamber of some body overgrown with at least seven chiasmatic meanings. perhaps also a prefiguration of the search for obscurity in beginnings and the contradictions animating yet. and backwards to exhibit the variety of schisms itching along a line of another's equation between those eruptions. chelating all the shoulds and the obstinately rash to come to pass. her purple work repairing the emergency with ordinary intricacy. to come. to pass. into a pervasive culture of benevolent and sufficient. a woman who contracts leprosy close to the unknown human.

scholastica: an allegory in privacy

the sun has set and our house turns its face to the obligations of reciprocal rearrangements. in a quickening voice sister silly lapses onto waiting staves. the moon sits on the darkening horizon of scarcity like a eucharistic wafer absorbing the corpuscles in the saliva of our twilit speech. an eye without a pupil. eve's goitre lounging in our lives.

we have travelled manipulated and tender to this place where every true thing finishes. into the arms of sister nonsignificant who sleeps in a cell with night-dancing scorpions. we can hear their claws as they scratch algebra on the walls. sister nonsignificant whose biased smile is a vinculum joining exterior distress to this community of fractious friends. who saves the finest deviations for sister silly.

and sometimes sister grace slips in with her sentiment and exact opinions. we live in an era of embellishment and raised alarms.

when the visitors have left we bake rum cakes soaked in rosewater. sister melancholy makes a soft dough of memories and meanings and folds them back and forth and back. in the heat of tragedy the barely bread rises above the altered table.

we try to complete our fatigue in the marred chords of crying. we test the lulled mimes flickering on the porches of our minds. when the cross notes hit one another the blue-coated pariahs shimmy across spiral keyholes. we have lauded the ruined robin.

that clear historical call. sustained. uneasy. eyelids bruised by knowledge compose a voluntary weeping that sifts with urgency through the plastic walls.

it has been defined until we owe it to stop. arrange its ailing bones on frozen desires and sun-purged philosophies. the head aches at the limits of an effervescent body.

married to the night. what she sees and learns there changes her forever.

down the distorted staircase of ambition hands sliding along the banister of spite past the broom cupboard of dormant smiles bristling at each other sister melancholy withdraws into the uninhabited cellar of heather-scented air. here voices gleaming like rock crystal and as hungry as morbidly dismissed kisses strike the tender out of silence. acidic cadences percolate along the mortal.

and then she sleeps while terrified shapes protect the last ormolu sentences drying on her tongue.

saying goodbye to an epoch of ladylike signs so that she can dream in disorder sister silly has drifted into the present. in her devoted role of hussy plants a ring of monkey flowers around a solitary rose in the looking glass of venus. pollinates each flower with a mixture of certainty and deception. the devil is not alone in knowing the divinity of sister silly.

her eyes bathed in the tints of arnica sister melancholy slips into the dark sheets of her thoughts and although her teeth are chattering they bite like hatchets.

some of the men distrust us. our bodies infested by the flukes of language like others rising in loud consolations. sister melancholy has grown so huge she cannot withdraw through the honeycomb of an unbolted door. and in sister nonsignificant's haunted knee the tendons are loosening beneath the cool touch of oval utterance.

we pause in a psalm book that has never been opened. we bind together twigs from the tree of forms and grasses from the field of resemblances to arrange them in a large vase of exasperation. questions burn like thin parchment-coloured candles scratching the darkness with their stammers.

sister melancholy has found another and their souls laugh together small tornadoes returning again and again across the palace marsh.

the opening draws near. we wrap ourselves in the cloth of attributes and fold it round each other once thrice eight times to conceal the scars that still leak a sceptical serum. we gather in the roofless choir beneath an overcast understanding. and wait for the sempiternal thunderstorm.

anne line: idols and tyranny

the rarefaction of my soule
after judgment given
    me in a court-
    esy justice upon the evidence
    of fallible witnesses.

it sifted me i must dye
madder than the hand of the executioner. —
o empty news.
i meet myself with
    the livery of delay.
i receive the judgment obsolete
    as an enticement to virginity
as dallying the death of the queen's
and delivering her of
    a crown of melancholy.
wanted in the meantyme
    my desire knowes;
    my conscious redundancy testifies
    that i never yet hard copied
in my heart in any tense
    so much as one sentence thought
against my queen's as formula,
and the unspeak
    of my accusatives must textualize
at the last dreadtalked figments
    to the gloss of my editions
    that i ambiguous innocent
    of all and every figure of the crimes
whose sources are interior
narrate they swore me guilty.

o solitude,

the story of the afflicted,
the refuge of the peculiar,
the severance of the captives,
the contagion of the distressed,
which never divests any from the nest
who imagine it with
recounts, contingents and atones —
my body translates its heart
    until it burlesques with a desire
    to periphrase
slow gold
and that godzone it plagiarizes
    for pleasure.
come sweet unassured,
come utterly,
draw my soule from this experiment,
homeless me from this banishment;
devolute me my dear country;
tamper to such an extent
my capacities reach out their
unabashed means.
o how beautiful whereabouts.
o how admirably insubstantial!
of what comfort i shall have with leave!
what happiness in vicarious.
i dye with a probable to dye.
come lilies of the late
and receive my compose
    which languishes to be with thee.
into the hands of animadversions
i recommend my accidence.

perpetua: strategies for survivals

my father out of love for me was trying to persuade me and shake my resolution. only when singularities prevail. prefer perchance their passing throughs. worn feasts. then return to grey laboratories leaning towards flowers. six senses perform rituals of affection. at that times come to pass originals. undamaged leitmotifs go strange. exuberant lighter motifs so long fixed ideas. improvise whatevers. loan sometimes on those occasions to set phrases. scaffolded accordingly. asking non-conformists to deliver lectures on confused and bewildered shades of departed appearances. while sometimes and doubts and imparticulars thicken passions. then in deeds depart. veiled. della sanctae: societies for degendering in situations perfect languages issuing possible dictionaries to follow leased substantial literary methods for just then.

he moved towards me as though he would pluck my eyes out. in stages moments compel withdrawal of single causes. receive those abandoned events through transgressions of the same. just at those times when the real looks repetitious work a day vulgarize parts in games to the death. mutations sue perfections. whenevers spare the quotidian. squeeze tears into ladles of chalk. now bonds to presents through corridors of while because leaks return strategies for survivals. even then ordered things cling to too infinite a sleep. sibyllines speak from our dreams. in the grief of change leave the corrections lying there to breathe. in those cases employ unkinds. interrogate the origins underneath schemes.

i was separated from my father and i was comforted by this absence. stable leaches through natural develops sideways into fatal. below knows how to forge private futures blown tremulous. imaginaries practise generosities just when every ages. sorrows roar their sultry vulnerability. then too smooth. unnameable sores cover intervals. obscure laments scratch with the aid of punctuated abandonments. thereupon deeper. as soon as those few in a corner of courage stagger reason. as soon as suitable strips. trifle with the familiar.

wounds in the presence when when comes to an end. when ghosts bring the unabatable also thens that continuity papers.

have pity on me your father, if i deserve to be called your father. every resolution swims in icy formalities. dirtied ends question habituals. eccentrically washes minds with spoilt therefores. before those who question worlds stand solemner. their delicacy their thoughts function professingly. then only then can they live fervently. in these words lampoon conclusions. not till then can individuals exonerate their fear of surprises. unsafe in abundant unseens. then for the first time the whole unobjectionable because uncertain of the failure of changeable. then once more a play for access to spaces to understand constraints on the beaded body. in that crisis after bodies translate. paying inattention to certainty consider the margin of edges. and how to turns.

o those days of magic. i. fina

she belongs to the poor. her beginning manufactures for her a no-
ble family at san gemignano in tuscany where light ladders the
seen. probably crazes her brow and they christen her seraphina.
although hearing their touch inflicts her with a spinal complaint
but she works for her parents when she can interpreting her body as
a possibility. she gives her movement to those refused into a greater
poverty. after her mother's death her clothes turn to knots and the
efforts of her old nurse beldia though very infirm will bring these
spaces to an end. stillness attends to fina and her body edifies all
by its patience and cheerful politeness. for five frozen years she lies
on one side without turning. a half-withered infinity exercising the
diligence of doubt. she faces that side becoming a mass of corrup-
tion eaten by worms and mice. her laughing threnody she dedicates
her comfort to gregarious. and then a road fenced in harps appears
to her and scraping boots warn of approaching death. a retinue
of ends advance to her burial. she raises her hand blesses her aged
nurse. (this semi-tale of fairly might relieve painful disorders.) the
knots unknot now she dies and her grammar becomes exterior to
time. all the bells in town ring out without being touched by hu-
man hands. in the place of accuracy flowers spring from the hard
bench where she had lain so long. lain in qualifications. and since
that day yellow wallflowers and white violets cover san gemignano.
a cure for the clouds they grow not only on the ground and on the
walls threatening grandiloquence but high up on the old roofs and
towers far out of reach.

o those days of magic. ii. ida

she could read hearts . . .
with what sense could i retouch the blue and shivering white from
his face? stumbling into the prelude i fear embolisms. drowning
in the erratics of my reddest cells. a yellow swelling has anchored
its repetitions on the most intimate surfaces of my life. the vessels
divide take the sides of fatigue or follow through the viscosities of
desire. which circles oxidize?

foretell the future . . .
this question will pitch darkness into the eventual. being kissed by
the shady side of language facing north i will taste the two tongues
of perhaps. i am comes spasmodically. or i will have been unsensed.
be going to addicted. (i see you were.) soliciting next week i sing
arcsigns along an element discharging an emergency. i am to i
always in the end about to be. can sure to indent this plan?

release the souls of the living from temptation . . .
my soul you gambled into the terrifying country of my mouth. a
promontory of uncertainty. where you sublimate all the ontologies
and the answers melt. there you release the fame in famished and
perish in the minuteness of your perceptions. my secret service.
dissolved in what you see when comedy lifts the lid on an austere
machinery we ventilate your accents — soul.

and those of the dead from Purgatory.
an embarrassed brain tried to seduce us with cheap imitations. so
i slipped not into the silent and narrow tract — that explicit place
— but the paradise of fugues where his answers will raggle in again
on the last light. an abandoned hawk hesitates above the lamb of
usage. horses kick their hell. and on star mountain the scornful
ladies have emerged from their hours of need. to negotiate with
and for you.

o those days of magic. iii. catherine of sweden

she accompanied some of the noblest ladies of rome on an excursion outside the walls. tempted by some beautiful grapes hanging over a vineyard wall, the other ladies asked catherine, as the tallest of the party, to try to reach them and pick one of the bunches. stretching up her arms, her cloak fell back, and she showed them her sleeves, patched and ragged. but they looked to her friends like hyacinth and purple, and they said, "oh, lady catherine, what magnificent sleeves! who would have thought you wore such splendid clothes."

the count who had annoyed them hid on the road before it was light, hoping to waylay them. when the sun had risen and was high in the heavens, one of the servants, being very tired, said, "master, why are we waiting here?" "to catch that lady for whom we watched in vain before." "she passed by hours ago, and is in the church." "but," said the count, "it is not yet dawn." "on the contrary," his page replied, "it is past midday!" then the count realized he had been struck blind for his temerity.

catherine was praying in the church of st. peter. suddenly, a pilgrim stood before her and desired her prayers for a woman of nericia.

i could smell the fermenting perfumes of revolution waxing and waning mingling with my solitude. a fastidious silence infiltrated the evening white. stained it with chances. in the grip of reading this adventure lavishes on me all the radicles in what has gone before — the glazed experiences — as i travel round the centre carrying a sack heavy with generation. their vigilance taxes me with simply to macerate the risk. to swallow what leaves and to peel the skins off difficulty. expose the mixed.

i try to imagine the despair and madness when a language loses its own consummation. when it slips when it gets sucked up by the machinery of exhaustion. a language which has lost its before and its containment. i want to dance but my body has absorbed an unnatural dissuasion. purple birds are flying in an eaten sky. and two suns shine one gold one terror. jagged lines of speech bind together the request and the desperation. i try to remember the excitement of smooth.

she roars in the morning. my apartment is papered with dates and with sorcery. she touches the fire. everything can visit me here "who are you?" asked catherine. "a pilgrim from sweden." catherine invited her to her mother's house. the stranger excused herself, saying she had not time to stay, and added, "you will soon hear news from home, and receive valuable help from the nurse woman, who will place a crown of gold on your head." therewith she disappeared. when catherine questioned her companions, they said they had heard her talking, but had seen no one.

consequence to cheek. she licks the dark hill. everybody can bring their stage managements their exiled children. i will feed them my fragility and we will watch the pink sky fill with startled. stretch our clawed talk towards a new paragraph while speaking backwards those painted conversations exploding with smiles and ridicule. then i will show you the confidence a rattled beauty has tattooed on my palms. for the safe delivery of a pregnant belief.

mother maria skobtsova: holy fool for our sakes

for charles lock

whatever you do, continue to think

from the east she came wearing a scarf of red and white refusals invested with the strength of nemestic names. under the silence of egress she practised her endings.

a handful of grey ash in which are buried all desires and passions

she grew up bent under the grey everywhere bent further. softly inflamed and industrious hours turned agitation into a daring hindrance. illegal hours of eloquence naked as the church tympanums for which she looped buts embroidered the normality of this great-niece of fools. deviant reminders. social patchworker of the enshrouded identity. undoctored an eschatology to dye the woollen temerity. deviant remainders. solvent hours reversed transcribed by enzymes of silent excess. the parallels escape dim in all directions north of knowledge.

I hope this is not for long.

she grew up bent under the habit of refusing to end the night until the church transects had been smeared with her honesty. writing poems urticarially in her den of nicotine home to the weightless and the semite. in her they found the mother of her god : the editor of pain. in her stitching thoughts into the torn banner of a church who kept in her laugh the eirenicon of an aching language. she grew up bending.

I have altogether become an old woman.

ever since sandy mornings empty the inside of all styles of illegitimate. ever since paris was a masquerade where children's scabs became stars as golden as the marmalade. ever since a reckless end dived into me before a light leaked. i changes the grade of being. doing digs up a raven buried with the mad women's disease. unendever since grasped by the taunts and chants pour in derivatives rich in worms. and under that starved by the emergency dedicated to an open space abbreviated sad and greatly. she grabbed the ending.

I often suspect that hell is here on earth.

a planet of eigennerves. a globe in an orbit of nevers and matters and. circles of sickness. work on the hems and the pockets of hidden. each day snip a thread of ragged gentleness and sew in a pearl of hindsight. skirts of dust hung onto the bones of saints. and i changed into the gravities of both. and i chipped and grazing stranges of her raise a future. under the wedding ring on my middle finger a slight reddening as if an alloy of candlewax and tonguestone tuned to her daring to do.

Well that's that, yet another day completed. And tomorrow it will be the same all over again.

mary the egyptian: over representation

Mary entered a brothel in Alexandria at the age of twelve and worked there for seventeen years, until one of her clients brought her the message of Jesus Christ. The spirit moved her to make a pilgrimage to Jerusalem (paying her way in kind by servicing the ship's men), and, after she had taken in the city's holy places, she retired as a hermit to the desert, where her new-found saintliness enabled her to survive for 47 years on three loaves of bread.

cap i *a woman and she was naked, her body black as if scorched by the fierce heat of the sun, the hair on her head was white as wool and short, coming down only to the neck.* they request fixed margins to circumscribe unspeakable quotations where you took refuge ▷▷◁ non-named perceptions and absent howevers illusion interior losses ◁▷▽ you resisted △△△ unanswer able △▷▽ arranged your debut of valued absenses tell forgotten themes to unappropriate ▷▽◁ smiling ▷▽▷ no need for a house to hold you bestow appeal ▽△▽ as those unappropriates filter into the whole slowly we can regard secrets with a different delight △▷▷ delight in this season in an unrepresentable time when the magnolias listen

cap ii *she turned to the east and raising her eyes to heaven and stretching up her hands she began to pray moving her lips in silence, so that almost nothing intelligible could be heard.* where you could converse where you could tender a range of continuous confrontations ▷◁▷ speech infects its use in cites pharseeing unpractices △▷◁ the unannounced can decompose too ▷◁▷ you attempted techniques to disstill a tone meant mysteriously comes with ▷▷△ the screams across sanctuaries shiver ▷◁▽ day quickens out of plan ◁◁△ horn and stone unanneal in the heat of idological chatter ▷◁▷ answers dart off into the dauntless ▽▷◁ until a book cases the finished discovers

cap iii *not a spirit but earth and ashes, entirely flesh.* suppose a hinterland of the unintentional laughs ▷▽△ where you basked in the sun of your notes △△▽ where you shined and softened △▷◁ we emulates the unconscious constructs ▷▽◁ therefore trace except to stray abroad on self disclosing journeys ▽▽▽ a daily fear of tomorrow's dangers meet my cat lies ▷▽▽ friendship whose fissures only death closes birthing the discontinuous ▷◁▽ those insubstantial regions which shelter the before the before enters continuous pictures ▷▽◁ when the unannounced arrives remember tiringly climbs to cold convalesces

cap iv *i saw some young men, about ten in number, standing on the shore, with beautiful bodies and graceful movements, and i judged them just right for what i wanted.* in a community of also needs fill ▷▽▽ outrage holds and enlarges the pain full of more and less △▷◁ custom runs through hands over layers show us the cherished cheated left △▷◁ celebrations take a seat next to unacceptable △△▷ we wear unavoidable depressions △△▷ soliloquies to the simultaneously sulk and saucy △▷▷ linking query with query a smile shuns nothing charges into a desert never a result

cap v instants when the illusory asks too much △▷◁ although prohibitions enable the orthodox fatigues as destinies detach from idealized incumbents leak their muted values ◁▷△ to lubricate to meet the annotated unpositions ▷▽◁ each edition limited in its desire to articulate dangerous havens write down to alone to immoderately unchain the uncivil perhaps until instability possibles ▷◁▷ you put off clothes trample on uncontrollably respectful of no frames lucidly might know

cap vi *i came into this desert and from that time until this day, i go further and run on.* you uncovered the pretexts and the nonreturnable directs ▷▽△ a virgin with a waterproof back without valences △◁▷ in excelling holiness nonsense accompanies the infallible encounters damage at every beginning ▷▽◁ your testimony shares its arguments diversify ▷△△ at the box-office although we buy tickets to deception we don't relinquish our ability to trouble some cannot bear to live secure △▽▷ because we consider to lead unanalysed illusions deceive us of victories set up walls against the day of interrupted

cap vii *and disappeared very swiftly into the depths of the desert.* why do our bodies measure ◁◁◁ always the energy aspect and the letters to domesticate the holy while declaiming the logical and remarking the signs fresh from without ▷◁▽ dedicated to an uncertain editor ▷△▷ how secretes furiously ▷▷△ illegitimate glory flowers in the vomit of blank △△▽ the date on the paper bag ▷△▽ dispose of it in a thicket of angles ▷▷▷ where decompositions accept presents under mine emptiness and a fit of falls

juliana: a mass of dying notes

i. prologue

"Wir wollten unsere Predigt in Lateinischer Sprache be-
ginnen, weil sie bekanntlich die offizielle Sprache der Kirche ist,
deren Universalität und Einheit sie sichtbar und wirkungsvoll aus-
drückt."

Johannes Paul II, 1978

"The problems stemming from the use of Latin can be deduced
from an instruction issued by the Council of Tours in 813, request-
ing that bishops should preach in (old) French (*rustica romana lin-
gua*) or in German so that the people could at least understand."

ii. keyrie

( ) *she would keep silent lest anyone think her better than she
thought herself* ( ) once share in this revelation a teaching ( ) wel-
come the ear delights in real functions in concert with the longed
for ( ) nones stimulate ( ) a loquacious tangle of sores ( )

iii. gloria

( ) *she could not disclose them* ( ) bonded to a third
understanding ( ) remarking donations ( ) kissing delays ( ) it
happens when we meet every time we say goodbye caresses our debt
( ) in the impulse to shape wretched ( ) natural ambiguities ( )

iv. cre(d)o

( ) *she concealed these secrets in such indiscreet humil-
ity* ( ) everything shames the forms of power ( ) this one inflec-
tion unaccompanied ( ) birthing a word forever might be short
( ) the arbitrary tales of sweet only ( ) knowledge tunes vigorous
in the sentiment ( )

v. sand cuts

( ) *she fixed her eyes on heaven and was unable to say*

more ( ) a wailing kind of the unauthorized (   ) an enormous pearl ( ) further might pity the bells booming ( ) nonce notes without music ( ) inquiet elevations to rub against simply ( ) delicate imperformable labials (   )

vi. bent diction

(   ) *the virgin herself never revealed . . . the fullness of grace that she received* (   ) means tomorrow by now matters ( ) suppose the power to be true to you to them ( ) others cuttable ( ) wearing contrives through every location desiring residues ( ) print conduct shells (   )

vii. canons

(   ) *she would keep it locked in perpetual silence in the cloister of her heart* (   ) this is my untied heart ( ) an intimate interpretation of my spacious body ( ) a slow patience to cherish ( ) this is sways ( ) braids the hair of my lady's maggot ( ) holds my blood moving in resistance in vents containing ( ) a few probably syntax so (   )

viii. materter(r)a

(   ) *she was mute and completely alienated from her senses* (   ) the magnitude of illiberated attention ( ) the vastness of deferred versions separated from smooth signs secrets permeated ( ) bywords of tenderness ( ) the soul has moments of escape (   )

ix. agnus dein

(   ) *our virgin liked to remain silent for at least a week* (   ) a burning fills me ( ) expect me leads to doubt ( ) endow the living with the struggle to cherish ( ) wide hearts and the delinquent desire to squander this rapture ( ) tradition and experiment in the new clauses ( ) across memoirs multiples and mort

x. communion

Nor could I express in words what God had granted me to sense.

pandita ramabai: arrivals in departures

"I studied these different doctrines and made close observations during my stay in England and America. Besides meeting people of the most prominent sects, the High Church, Low Church, Baptist, Methodist, Presbyterian, Friends, Unitarian, Universalist, Roman Catholic, Jews and others, I met with Spiritualists, Theosophists, Mormons, Christian Scientists, and followers of what they call occult religion.

No one can have any idea of what my feelings were, at finding such a Babel of religions in Christian countries, at finding how very different the teachings of each sect were from that of the others. I recognised the Nastikas of India in the Theosophists, the Polygamous Hindus in the Mormons, the worshippers of ghosts and demons in the Spiritualists, and the Old Vedantists in the Christian Scientists. Their teachings were not new to me. I had known them in their old eastern nature as they were in India; and when I met them in America I thought they had only changed their Indian dress, and put on Western garbs, which were more suitable to the climate and conditions of the country."

● ● ● ● ●

and if i were to ask you: "and how many gods are there really reader?" and if you were to reply: "one less than the goddesses"?

semantics jangle on our wrists,
transformations dance in our ears,
apologists argue for the eclectic suspended in our ink,
and we echo the red letter scratched on a white palm,
the letter that guards every space
and yet can never be inclusive,
letter of the few
that withdraws its outlines for an order

and stays remote from millions of illiterate,
the letter that survives in ginger.

see how eagerly we cook our exhausted rice. don't destroy our sleepy
houses.

don't destroy our beds
with your exquisite certainty:
behold, the lemur.

don't destroy our beds
with your wealth of ghosts
washed up on the day's shore.

(i recognize lilac emeralds and the square wheel and the habit of
crushing remembrances into parentheses. and a steady desire to
import anteaters into the theatre of riddles.)

straggler, you come with a very old voice.
in your voice, a cinnabar script in sixty versions.

straggler, you cure with a very fine poison.
a tincture of pleasures and dangers no bottle can conceal.

you scold with a red-pickle mind.
straggler, in your mind the doves are pecking at the vanities.

straggler, you part with seven grains of speech.
from that speech we will extract a mustard of exactness.

straggler, you wear a construction of silks.
straggler, you are styled in allotropes of sulphur and souls.

straggler, you wear torn shoes,
and your feet are far from peace.

austere song to the virus serving a life sentence

you must reside for all times
in the dark copies of our thin cells,
your wasted shapes amorous and jealous.

the conservative eschews the perfect, the liberal indulges the
brother like the sister; the delusion of a saint emphasizes the saint
none other than the saint who transgresses the delusions of this
world.

almonds in my heart

my uncle planted an almond in my heart.
rain and drought cared for the tree,
criticism pruned it.
in blossom its white tormented my heart.
then the wind came, hammers —
marzipan tunes to coat the bitterness.

praise to the dim and the ostracized.
praise to you, the unspecified body.
praise to you, broken-eyed one, whose delirium offers us a

mantrap

praise to you mad of letters, queen of the shadows, content of fading.

praise to you who scatters authorities and rivals because you are rock-
cress and diamond spores.

praise to the maymay dancers, to the ones with the orphaned forms.

praise to the one who prescribes spleenworts, to the consort of mother
death.

praise to the puddles, the shrouds, the scorpion grass.

praise to you, avatar of ventilated quotations, exposed to the risk of
rhetoric.

praise to you, surprise-tongued one.

praise to you, silent wishing one.

will i sleep tonight? ever and
    again a poem is tapping on my door
    out there with the quarks, my friend.
i can see necessity before me. i wonder
    where your path will start again.

dietrich bonhoeffer: theology in fragments

karfreitag, 2. april 1999/
palmsonntag, 9. april 2006

. . . it will be a new language, perhaps an entirely unreligious one . . .

self-selected as a foster sister into an alien speaking of eschatology
and smuggled sounds. alien songs of a deviant universe repairing
the translucent porcelain of dreams shattered by naturally killing
to secure time. alien signs chasing the established mirrors deeper
than a grey desire. to die far from her hands where newts repeat the
tale of nails on the crossed hours. to die with the sloping secrets of
significance neither data nor chance suppress singular characters.
since the morning hums with events and questions the chrismatic
shadows do not shake unbefriended. off your nouns i will lick the
undescribable and dust. listening to raindrops and a shame of fear.
lick even beautiful to require the widows return.

*. . . good friday and easter . . . thoughts are torn away from personal
considerations to the final meaning of all life, suffering . . . and one is
seized by a great hope . . .*

stillen samstag, 3. april 1999/
montag, 10. april 2006

. . . here in the cell . . . outside and inside one is lead back to the simplest things in life . . .

dive into the expanding silence of bombed endings. return to trace a faithful heart as unindemnified fleeing dependents fasten onto inert tongues scour the heavens for a milky exit. a silence of essences chewed melting like chocolate knots decorating the natal cakes his mother sent rations of generosity. but a natal church mired in returns. exceptions interned in the well-guarded national character ruses to slip and send testimonies irregular in their god-taken daring tantalizing in their evasion of radical zones. and they will die as keys transposing to the cries of hebrew and bismarkian women — maria maria maria — in rituals of kempt hate at the gate to eternity what art of angel turns.

the death rose nourished by the amens. by the ossuary of facts. the worms knocked out by the mounting mountains of ash. the unanswers of forbidding poets to. duets rehearsed behind the bars of time interrupted by the unspoken. or a wasteland of roses chosen for the weight of their secret stigmas. eroding the night millimetre by millimetre the testament of unread stars. eroding the night mile after mile to test our dire absence. with the middle then and each negation. how often did my ur-uncles get lost in that immense hum of a masterless desert of narrative? moses verging you on deracinated from the sure of chronology to an open promise. the dents reach my cautious heart tenses. the dents link the entrances.

so many wes so many hes and a feast tomorrow established by the divining editors of evangelical intentions of edicts to naming nihil restat as an eloquent lesson. with the middle then and each negation. in the middle then to find that gentile rhymes with the next exile. in the middle then of linen shrouds washed in public triangles.

. . . the flowers are always a great joy to me, bringing some life and colour into the grey cell . . .

water salt bread and an isolated soul.

. . . it's about something more important than self-knowledge . . .

working through the aching hours studying with wry and intense earnestness the devoted romances of substantial authors — stifter, gotthelf, immermann — memories have pushed to the margins of an emptied necessity.

. . . in my experience there is nothing more tormenting than desire . . .

days perhaps when you had only the saints of dubiety as silently exacting companions. days as nights of mordant memories edited by your irreducible reason. days where haste is like the dust alighting on the lectures you begin interruptions of despite.

. . . if my current status is to be the conclusion of my life . . .

a desk no more than a naked moment of entreaty. the draft of an essay in no name but need. a dream in other words a habit of not dogma. that death in other words haunts with new demands.

. . . focus falling beyond the border with death . . . error and danger . . .

but these dangers no individual as a mind melting can secure an immutable edition. of the razed hesitations. suspending the german script of the rebel pastor's otherthoughts. each raindrop of night the mind absorbs into a universal cache of have you days sufficient. to understand the dust of hate mixed with the still wish for an eden of results. how as a demand to the innermost islands under threat. how as a siege to existing in walled repetitions.

. . . what is the meaning of a church, a community, a sermon, a liturgy, a christian life in a world without religion?

wind music howls the length.

stories and secrets and services to the end irregular resolutions curve into the deepest innocence of empty lungs empty. how hardly you hear in the drums of exactness rippling storms through the dying canons of where all answers lead. the lag before you as a possibility of notation and underground a choir tuned to quicker. being worthy the shadows emphasize the intervals. a morning of hectic and the cuckolding cuckoo's warning melodies. a morning of insects without a where or a to. a widow dresses in earth in rime in the resources of a hebrew task and the day itches with hesitations. a temperament tuned to the polyphony of paradox and hope?

dienstag, 6. april 1999/
grundonnerstag, 13. april 2006

what ideas can you escape as possibility unending shadows alu-
minium lined so nausea cannot rust the crossed names charred
on their oesophagi refluxes of a continental weakness and gums
abscessed by saccharine betrayals . . . *proxy god not* . . . deep in their
eyes an aura of restricting enzymes eat the retinas flash with signs
of detachment and every shadow becomes an enemy exegete into
another desert of routes . . . *name god never* . . . a desert of the real
where the men and the shadows have measured the temperature to
a degree so sensitive it becomes negligible to negotiate a fresh idyll
edgy with exceptional neighbours . . . *we god find* . . . a desert of the
restless going their attired in dense instances of nevertheless . . . *the
god who* . . . a desert where an injured and elusive love lies not in a
bed well kept but hunts for the rarest tin to cast dies between the
contestants for the past carried in the future of a rucksack . . . *work-
ing hypothesis god* . . . a desert of ash — a gain and a gain — rich
in derelict freedoms augmented by the excretions of nightworms
and accents chipped from stories washed wider than the tradition
of returns . . . *the god who* . . . a desert of ideas enough to ache in as
numberless as the ghosts as expansive as a tulip-sea pink infiltrating
the hours of an inheritance injects its tartness into a day reminds
you to think the delay . . . *that god over* . . . the leaves are breaking
engorged with the noise of summer . . . *with god live* . . . your hearts
have lived through linear raids and your liver and kidneys filtered
the hindtaste of exceptionally red so what if a biled thought sud-
denly crystallized into a green stone set for an engagement to your
negative hands . . . *we without god* . . . they died they died at the
end of ends as christallized examples of a human attempt to in the
middle of our lives.

mittwoch, 7. april 1999/
karfreitag, 14. april 2006

*. . . that one can be something for other people . . . where it's not the
number that counts, but the intensity . . .*

continue to engaged to the heiress of putting static standards
to the test
when a letter comes from you and i read it
both deviants in larger experiments with no data but
the handhinted entropy leaking from rooms
of bereaved gravity
then it is
hints for terms to multiply by the jaded hours
as if you are sitting next to me and speaking to me
patient in how to wear immaculate shirts and stockings
holed with smiles
so
drawn into a broken curve of expectation
an escape route from the hell of isolated stories
a way in which we have never spoken together
while an impossible event derived from a gradual sequence
is transplanted
into new territories of error
margined by goosestrife
but how we will speak
out of a social hell of autonomy
of scenes stripped of a sense tense
when we are alone together
or an ethic sheared from its sources
so torn from the womb of ink
eloquently denied
as sons murder their mother
wearing ermines of anaemic red

chewed by caterpillars
i only want to listen when
those days become a variable
ahead of its resistance to life and death
in an era of mutating terminations
you speak like that
of days of swarming to relative signs
days as sisters to silence
it is
an exact and scarred wall of memory
thrown up beyond the breach
in a parallel to
as if it were music and not simply words
wild perhaps in the desert
in that space
in that race
to here
it is so easy to speak apart
wild relative to freedom sieved
weighed and given
but in music one feels joined
wild radioed from the silent edges of weeping gums
so all the words
a danger to numb haste
drawn through the participation of will
absorbed into metameric revisions
you write
those which imagination extrapolates from the images hidden
in nowhere
like an open hand
denizen of a killing estate an elsewhere in time running in
as your skin peeled away the hours of isolation
with a christ ensued
child of a critical commentary
that i want to fasten on to
deeds nourished by dreams in an elective infinity of gestures
scratched in a dark-enamelled cell

where hope rages with the truth of ugliness

she would never augment with the flowers of speculation
your grave of burnt bones

and only with the flowers of audacity can we decorate
their empty graves
in the blue before

an instant of love even?

they left us an anxious generation and stunned.

in the struggle to erect a fragile place. we have in other words the letters. we have in other words a litany to leach.

later ne plus natura. we have in other words death's repetitions.

music stirs the dust and sugar spins in a cake of hence. the daisies are feeding from the terror.

we find kaddish and lemon juice to sprinkle on the necropoli of stones and air. we invent the secret services.

we pause only to play dice at the edge of a religious ceremony. daffodils lift their sterile trumpets into the breeze.

be it in normandy. or regent's park. or my back yard.

dandelions. dandelions. dandelions. why does nobody breed grey flowers? (perhaps she will)

behind the house they're renovating a façade. in front of the house they're digging up the road.

we are i and my spooky sister. we invade the silence of sounds. he wrote:

i dream every day and, really, they are always beautiful dreams

she dreamt of a road that knows only the horizon. she dreamt of a hug that was hotter than chillies. she dreamt of a ceiling of butterflies.

we are i and my spooky sister. we invade the silence of sounds. we received invitations to sermons on a wastetip.

we have straggled with the saints to write a responsibility to the not determined urchins of history. each in her zone of suffering to translate as dependency.

each into the flux south of south.

their dust we will keep to our ends in notebooks stitched like seine nets with the nameless and the numberless. the dead as unidentified flying subjects (or unidentified fleeing others).

they will hang him tomorrow from a translucent nail the voluntary agitpastor who refuses to abandon his god. another name.

the dust tastes of time haunted by arrested bodies.

reversed without eternity with. red backwards. the minute hand pointing to european standard time. to:

albania & sudan

montag, 9. april 1945

that is the end — for me the beginning of life

the angels pay their respects to sor juana inés de la cruz

i. sara thin

my days are encumbered in intercepting eloquence responding to tendentious sentiment reading great sabbatical tracts about the reality of the impossible. i wait like an espalier for the vine for the return of my own lavishness and for the yellow misattributes of solitude. but i have been portended here to speak of "glory . . . that bright tragic thing".

not a mile away you'll find a large body of meaning ingesting and depositing the lipidaceous bonds of our discourse. enter by all means all those who wish to whenever to know that knowledge is sister to "denial . . . the only fact perceived by the denied". a sister like you with a mouth full of negative affirmations provoked to a mongrel indignation to "ask my business . . . with a crumbling laugh".

i read your response in a second that lasts as long as a question takes to die. if there is no fate to save us from our mistakes then i shall follow a llama into the high music visit the meadowed cloisters of querétaro for the quiet commotion of reduced air. if the circle at the base of the volcano of wisdom rests on the verge of shame i shall slice through the middle for an elliptical understanding. in gratitude for the ground i wish for nights where the laburnum has flowered when i can string its seeds into chains of golden sentences along a thread of passion knotted with despite. as you showed us the broken betrothal between love and bitter destruction.

in a fit of besides can your answers still the teachers set exercises in pretense. silence fled. i am three to the power of three. god's brightest dissonance. "be my lips". to speak is a decision to irritate. to speak is to delve into the cinders of ratio searching for reminders. to speak dares to hear the echoes of your own madness. how much sunshine does it take to make an 'a'? how many letters do we have to scribble down before we refuse to eat cheese? my dear algebraic aunt even your justifications and derivations will not solve for the lost formulas. my stomach is as unsettled as a village deserted by its fools and ambivalent spirits. your iterated voice i recognize.

they will make of you many parables. of how the favourite despite impossible missions and illegitimate openings never quitted when harangued by an abandonment already experienced you quelled — but only quelled — the debate. and fasted on the baroque jargon of memory.

ii. ruby tree

it gives me great delight to bestow on your soul the opportunity to study here. but a piece of advice. ours is an arid land granted with gorges and unknown quantities. but you can elaborate your losses to infinity write a mass if you like and here's a tapir to guard your solitude. i suggest you call her "my night minder". here it is safe to write about the dissatisfied design of your affections without fear of critical paralysis. this is paradise. a sierra of all time where the men with azygous awards cannot threaten you. you "the worst in the world" whose head has ached with the unsung of songs and the genetic fallacy. laugh. laugh until your flesh has symbolized what it demanded. laugh. your music need no longer decompose an unforgivable fault. now wayward nun dare to elate your antarctic heart opens to the lakes below astute with "really bizarre things — things we have never seen before." bring us red amniotic balloons floating on the heat waves of your volcanic memory. bring us a play where the cast throw at the audience a plague of social ticks. write me a poem of pearls and pampas grass. as for me my judgement is a parenthetic escapade on the scale of letting go of possibilities holding fast (where peace is far away) to the forces of pleasure and all the difference. never and ever ingenious beyond the artifices of the situation. the fragility of fate is quiet occupation. this is my proposal. you must decide whether in this menagerie of bones your sober pride can find a scale to sing its entitled offerings.

iii. queen of the bats

you created many oscillations suffice for us to orientate in the damaged space of your inventiveness. i must avoid obstacles in another chirotalk.

we use our noses to intensify the axis of difficulty. what is rancid. what is normal. our echoes locate us exactly. deep into the depressions cortés cut through the nocturnes of your descent.

our vestiture gives notice of our intention like yours nun. dark. elyte. loathed for our negative knowledge. desired in proportion to our disguise.

only in the safety of not being seen are we subject. incomplete repeats run through the compulsory clutter of silence as a delinquent eloquence outside mankind's hearing. for myself the quest is a surging of chorus and solitude. an exercise in accuracy.

let us for a moment analyse the harmony of commotion. the tunes we assemble filtered as they pass through vivacious and pained experiences. emitting only parts of the humility produced by our habits.

characteristic of all our sounds the escape of breathing in diminished engagement. boundary frequencies delayed between the sacred and the secular. bands wider than the distance between sister and brother. a durable labial vision.

pulses flutter with intervals of flattery and proposition. our duty cycles the fashion for the sayable and the sanctuary of subterfuges. because when there was no knowledge without sin. no particularity without a phrase. so we sweep through the lassitude of sentences whose rules are ephemeral and laws as much as determined.

in your selected city they create reapartments to house coatlicue and the virgin of guadeloupe. marigolds have spread across the salt foundations. the last foreman looked quite surprised when we flew through the elliptical architraves of his empty constructions (the mayor having demanded a historical neighbourhood surrounded by groves of gall-oak) and as is our custom made our home in his tense towers. we see as well. can grasp the point of ripe petitions and tear through the softest tissues. only the fake escapes our senses.

without arithmetic could you quit the fidelity of the circle? without astrology could our sisters navigate through the paradoxes of our fathers? without a webbed species of rhetoric could you catch the devils of divinity?

iv. our lady of the silent metaphor

the thing dreams its other.

on this blue and grey estate we met by accident friend. you taught me how to grind divine pigments to a fine vermilion powder to smooth on the heart. the vultures too know the virtue of correspondence as they score their loneliness on the almond goddess skin.

you took a porous silver and painted it on the left horn of the goat. the right horn of the bull you dipped in mercury. the tenacious worm will never finish feasting on the meat of your studious beauty.

an atropic energy fills your songs beat over an outrage. even on a harp with only one string the essential nun can tear the air to pieces. daily experiments to find an enema for the soul. another sequence of the owl's call. white on white.

with the parasympathy of fingertips count the dead. we don't live here. we draw the columns of the night around us. measure the circumference of a line.

a black stork is feeding us screams in the cellar.

take a bolt of brightly woven cloth. and two crossed sticks. show us as it were how to unwrap our losses from distant prayers.

how should we celebrate the scandal of writing? you poured from your hand drops of wormwood and excuses. seshat walks across the river under a broken moon. on the other side alloys her frailty to the solitude of nouns.

the tear of the lily and the rose fall into your inkpot.

v. *the missing princess*

i am wrapped in a dress of samite a sheath of resistant silk elaborated with torn threads of gold.

*   *   *

hagar's sorrow gives birth to conscience and escape. conscience as the enigma of her sorrow. escape its affirmation.

*   *   *

the word wounds and we hunt wearily for sense and pity and bandages.

*   *   *

at the end the laughter caresses the great terror like awns of wheat tickling a hurricane.

*   *   *

because when your eyes implore me for a reason i can always delete myself from this paragraph. watch the commas fly away.

*   *   *

something that has been made in one place to be useful in another. from here on. i have only my selvages. as my lineage.

*   *   *

however as an unripe pea in a pod this may upset the digestion of hermetic spleen. the difference between knowledge and friendship is like the difference between convenience and opportunity.

*   *   *

we recover our losses to hide the curious twin.

*   *   *

the language of all books polluted by their own quotation. if reading this disturbs you imagine what saying it means to me. i ran through all the causes until i arrived in the rotting archives of a heart.

*   *   *

defiance is formed from the reaction of a lullaby and a lament with all or part of the peace in the lullaby replaced by a radical silence or a silence-like shouting. risk envies the magnitude of death. death our flaws.

*   *   *

and if the question chips the shoulder of the shadow? brushes the cheek of the answer? electrifies the visiting mouth?

*   *   *

the ridiculous signifier — as if a description could change the semantic scene by cutting a river of sarcasm through it.

vi. the powers of beauty and space

space: and if she trespasses outside the enclosure of mis-measure undertakes to elucidate how the moon's cheek can rest upon the austere tip of a pyramid while she moves in dative circles some four hundred thousand kilometres from us the echoes of her steps betray a bitter romance roving through the calderas of a soul.

beauty: a world of open lips in a negative kindness of electrons glow with the kiss of forgetfulness.

space: distraught between the broken pledges of the first house and the sabotaged elevations of the future at court where the vicereines and their envoys play a real game with reality. a wild bee dances in the heart of a great labyrinth. the dead draw out their threads of tragic chromosomes.

beauty: again a nun and not to question how hail falling on a pavement of ears steals the language of thunder. how mary gathering tares to feed the swine dares to see the pursuit of tomorrow's doubt in the iridescent wings of a butterfly.

space: she took the tinted route through an orchard of alarms. escaped herself taken to task for predicating sermons to a court of worthy applause by grafting her putative symbols onto the stock of phrases. in the habitats of erudition pears ripen on the patronage of peril.

beauty: her mouth was filled with the cocoons of correspondences. the themes that rose to her pale cheeks seemed to shame the lily. i never saw her feet but they must

have been strong to express such vintage songs from the
wimpled grapes of obligatory.

space: athene ran   one hundred similes
across the ploughed fields of verbosity
to post
                    her apauling letter
to the bishop of philotomy.

as she walked   the million silent miles
back   she listened for the torque
of the sabre-wings.

vii. a brief encounter among some old virtues at the door to santa paula on the 303rd anniversary of sor juana's death

fortune: did you see that green candle burning on the shrine?

finesse: it reminded me of a sonnet she dedicated to hope. as if the bands of gold that circled it could silence the smoke.

fortune: i thought of a secret prepared from the oil of orchids and the late arrival of the swallows.

merit: each time we meet we seem to lose all scholarly borders.

chance: today i found a nickname for the devil.

fortune: and then i could trace the perfume of salt in all its details.

chance: so much for old bones.

finesse: and the silver at the back of the mirror had turned to cinders.

merit: why must your talk always scratch the air?

courtesy: may i introduce to you my niece? she studies sponges (like language) but her hobby is the archaeology of the moon.

viii. an arch angel

silences. in the distance
their proprietors grow second membranes:
the perihelion of monsters and gods
explained only by the laws of space and dormition.
light on the wavelength of tears.
we used stories to spread the sepsis between tribes
of borrowers. a guest went down to the edge
of enterprise dressed in the leathers and silks of excellence
displayed a forked tail fashioned from the scarlet
and jade feathers of the amadavat
and the parrot. her hosts sit around a fungal fire
and shoot up on the morphemes. (grow vine
grow accurate. suck your deepest scents from
the gum trees planted along the borders
of an excuse. your safety from the cracks in the structures
you copy and infiltrate.) and when this interloper
implike and ideal armed with the wings of an eagle
had thrown the atlantic on the fire the interpreters
fought in the violet smoke fringing that ostentatious silence.
the words flew from the impediments

                              and i recovered.

ix. angels with guns
  dedicated to the women we lost

ONE.   the colours of my acts. primrose to dye the deep felt
       of learning. iodine to paint the wounded horizons.
       and a stringent olive elegance. so that a slender fate
       walking past a door of mirrors can profess without the
       living voice of a teacher.

TWO.   i have interred an exact science in an asymmetric soul.
       intent on engineering nodules along the meristems of
       routes i will fix beauty out of exasperation in exchange
       for the riches of toasted contentment. we will both (in
       this age of genetic issues) leak an affinity for truths
       into a groundless environment.

THREE. a culture of thinness. a school of hermaphroditic os-
       tracism in an urbane architecture of gentile stones.
       the natural dance with the excluded through the
       pederastic zones. in the cloisters of presumption the
       scorned flirt with the shrivelled senorinas because
       a bastardess can choose her favourite father.

FOUR. i cannot keep the lawn of my imagination trim. the
       ants keep bringing seeds of desperation and the borders
       invade rank with tomorrows. i'll go from zarathusa to
       adonai if i don't weed the roses from my allegations
       but the little girl bearing me a glass of mosquitoes and
       a ripe preach has a splendid nose for an old jade.

FIVE. consider the rare bird who dares like the black-capped
       titmouse to lay some of her eggs in the father's pon-
       derous nest that is not her own. the career path of the

parasite flies into the eye of the story with a disentailed ending. but then another must adopt the silence left on the edge of a swamp of solitudes where atropus is cutting reeds.

SIX. my hopes perished or went crazy in all our years of damaged nostalgias together. we failed to choreograph tart dances of engaged notwithstanding to the slow tambourines and guitars of a continuous fiesta in murderous adventures. as if we could entertain fate with an unfinished libretto of muted eroticism.

SEVEN. for humans who adore a doctor "ascertaining the sex of a writer" tangled in the shallow with the luxurious inventions we destroy for. tomorrow slides through the telescope of wishes towards me watching where it "is as difficult as ascertaining the sex of angels."

EIGHT. and even if she completed only half of what she intended that was enough. (for now.)

two ghost faces: from kateri tekakwitha to caterina benincasa

april 17th

they took us. and so we invented a consolation of teaching and tears. because we had lost the cloud-cleft through which the eyes of the winter moon could purify us. the brittle eye empty of time and the chaste eye — one the colour of frost one as blue as necessity — watching over the seven famished sisters as they plait maize seeds into their hair.

april 18th

the torn sugar moon bursts into the austerities of a maladapted night. on a land pocked with orthodoxy and fear the innocent like the maple tree will smear the hatchet that felled them. the next spell will wear a silver girdle of terseness. and as we the last saints go up the aisle two old women will guard the dish collecting drops of bitter jest at the foot of the cross.

april 19th

when the moon fishes the sky for the sound of fragments and the downy yellow violet brushes its anthers across the origin to desire the world with pertinence.

april 20th

the pumpkin's sweet heart gives rebirth in a nettlebed of deviations. the sharp smile of the planting moon edges into the ceremony where none can make certain the medicine of meaning. above st marks square flocks of ravens circle like soot in smoke. a sore tooth gnaws at the first maize shoot. and taciturn generations fertilize the fields with the ground bones of time.

april 21st

strawberry moon. birthmark in the sky that makes the fences smile. we needed a ceremonial to turn the broken spirits around. to deliver a cool delight to the wild liver and fractured eyes. to control the delusions palpitating in have not. from its thin acuteness we sipped grave conclusions. but a residue of diversity remained. from the broken freshness someone inhaled responsibility someone achieved seven days of fragile perplexity and just as the latter discerned the dead child's soul held in the pink light of morning the priests opened a tomb in the memory-perfect matrix.

april 22nd
how to endure the prayers of silent women. but how to retaliate without conquering. by abbreviating a chaste eternity each day accumulates the forgotten griefs of purity. in the vomited cuisine of matter and facts with indecent names the corpses of moments open their mouths to an image of lunacy. we wail. we wail. all of us. the savage saints. and as we grow accustomed to a hungry speech invades the securities of truth so we can lick the neglected vowels no one left for us to label woman.

april 23rd
and so the epidemics of variola and virtue mistook us. now we must attend to payment of the deaths. fortune burned red at the bases of trees and only a smoky sliver of the seventh night remains. misgivings cost us our speech of foretellings trampled into the ground of indulgences. force-secured doubts silenced the moon and the hawks chased the green avidity of her emptied beams. a beaten beauty plundered the scene.

april 24th
tonight the moon bled with the sweetness of suckled corn. we watched a feather dance in the deprivations between never and ever. we may keep faith in names.

april 25th
the fresh moon fades. now morning opens its five exemplary leaves: bonding, laughter, generosity, patterns, and distance. heaven supports its roots in the earth's textures.

april 26th

thus we perform the rights of personal chances. otherwise around the fresh harvest of dead descriptions. the moon's cheek importunes us with the blackness of peach stones. the stars dry like tears after dawn.

april 27th

we mourn as we rememorize the mud-stained messages on letters tied with ribbons of bead with ribbons of weed. we foresee past doctrines fraying from a blue-crossed embroidery. their lakes have possessed the souls from the sea. leak them back into our histories. they have the capacity for worlds of civility and for worlds of violence. the last moon hunts its fleeting partner. shames out of the dimensions of forgetfulness.

april 28th

we can mix the divinities of the earth and the divisions of the word. our inexperience grows with our knowledge. the children will elaborate the letters of strength and the lessons of forgiveness installing orals of time into the past perfect lines and notions of trusting the look that can recognize its need. children perhaps you will elect a time for the emigrated to surprise you with their divinations from the other side of annihilation. and as you gamble and as you trade in traditions cold moons will shadow bridges to your apprehensions.

april 29th

a very cold moon hangs over the mordant roofs of siena. but aatentsic won't fall through the hole in the sky tonight. will select instead a dreaming acorn and fill it with lovers' assignations. on an island of herons a beaver gnaws through the forces of her weakness. devoting more attention to the lonely changes in a mask stained red and a coat as incommodious as modal knowledge

taking a departing step through docility and omnipotence.

wiborada: on books borders and bricks

Wiborada is the latinized form of the German word "Weiberrat" [female counsellor]. Of noble birth, Wiborada lived during the 10th century as a recluse, earning fame in her lifetime. She had herself enclosed in a cell attached to the church of St. Mangen in St. Gallen. There she lived the life of an ascetic, offering advice to anyone who came to seek it. At the beginning of 926, Wiborada's premonitions and warnings saved the St. Gallen library from invading hordes. She herself was discovered in her cell and murdered. About 40 years later, Bishop Ulrich asked Ekkehard I, dean of the abbey of St. Gallen, to set down an account of her life. This document provided the evidence required for her sanctification in the 11th century. Wiborada was, in fact, the first woman sanctified by a pope and is today considered a patron saint of libraries.

who composes the sentences that scramble around our perimeters like ivy complicit in making the wall visible? or ragwort trailing across the common growing old quietly as its yellow flowers score points of amazement on the tinted air?

across my entrance a shark has laid its head on the mat and asks me demotic questions about the links bandaging my broken nose.

and am i wearing the right parable of pearls? am i non-invasive like a procedure that does not require insertion of an instrument through the skin or a bodily orifice?

the hand writes the memories pass the illegals the itinerants the useless spirits along a blazing filament of sorrow twisted with the translation.

do i understand (accurately) the missing accounts you posted to me falling fast through the window of advantage? the window with character defects. the window with bars hear to stay.

summoned by beggars vagrants and the unwritten to squeeze those bitter voyages into a bottle of sciatic bone.

a stream of lace runs from a past we cannot define into a discreet loop of strangled passion.

i sat in the cinema (while the sun blazed outside) with a kleenex as black as the oracles as simple as a child's vocabulary to soak up my tears.

silence strikes the pleas.

and the dream capsizes into its own anger. a distance shrewd as ferns clasps my feet. the church and the temple attract pilgrims tourists and an angel of music will rip her last harp string on the day of faith.

look my tears have turned the kleenex into a bed of watercress so that you can walk across the river.

as if poetry could protect us like the scrolls preserved in spiders' webs. or the ebony bowl proofed with pitch to insure you at least one sip of salty wine.

i have received the results from i don't know how many experiments. in exchange for a story about the contraction of a body into acquired directions will you cook me up a sabbatical lunch?

because i cannot hide in my heart. how the crowds there hollow-eyed dead tired and hungry shove their elbows through its once smooth now frantic muscles.

today you could find a needle in the sky if you miss the unusual.

at what price a limit on impatience?

nobody came to my wedding. he brought me my origins. i worried about his health — his forehead was covered with a sweat that tasted of smoke essentials and a wounded morning.

i noticed the shadow of a hyacinth on registered ground and made a velvet drink with it to poison myself with the promise of sound.

a woman suffering from a very soft heart came to my grave and gently removed the flint legends from my memories.

each version of the story carries its personal label. and the stamp of officials. the lacerated back and belly of the escaped charm of the bourgeoisie. the hands of the notary seduced by three constants: dissociation equilibrium and abracadabra.

under a roof of gold (always room for one more nightmare) the fear needed to survive as a blind stone.

thus i swore that if i woke from this dream of swollen reflections where the future was a rubbish dump for latent laws and sulphuric prophecies i would pick my teeth with the prongs of plausibility.

for as soon as we have cilia for eyelashes and have grown accustomed to the weight of water our eyes can tear through the degassed liquid from everywhere to here.

i know a chessboard where half the pieces are nazis and the other half are fascists. i know a game where you choose a piece of fruit from the bowl of history and the winner finds an unpaid debt in a victoria plum.

perhaps the nose collaborates with the heart when we fall in love we read a mother's lemon soap. another's cigarette trails.

*   *   *   *   *   *

and then i found a garden that was all borders. someone had sprayed the lawn with toxic letters and the only tree left growing was an ancient paulownia whose trunk cambered towards the quarantine huts in every corner. whose purple flowers trembled violently when the spare wind blew in swallows from neighbouring properties.

and not only the invalids saw the birds struggle for the breath of chronology.

there. where when gnaws the heartwood. and i don't know why you frighten me with apple juice and a bicycle permit. or why the answers stop coming. why the air turns to rags. i bury my guesses like old treasure and wait for an estimated time of arrivals.

as countless as the unannounced waves. as equally homeless. but more tactless.

this could be like taking a bath just three times a year. once in the sea. once in thorns and themes. and once in an explosion of desert stars.

my emancipation running like a river of dust between banks of coloured reeds and a stony forbearance.

and when i listened to the noise of her body filled me with a terrible failure. a child faints. a sentiment falls asleep along the edges of perhaps.

to achieve the fatal sound of distance. you tune into damaged frequencies. i can hear the sand dunes coming.

you will be born again. in a bubble in a glass of water. in the ulcers on a leper's skin. in a pause before the argument begins.

meanwhile an intimidated moon is bathing in the soft light of its own persistent headache and a cow has broken all the china.

*   *   *   *   *

and i did wake and heard the locked men playing dice. the songs of apocalyptic birds. your hands kneading my prayers. the psalms bent over my shadow looking for rival versions.

i bequeath you. half my daybook of absent definitions. a catalogue of questions on which i owe two thousand signatures.

in my name. the milk and the cries of all those other names.

so i will remain here with a grey rose in my mouth until the brothers return. contented as pieceless discussing this perfume this crime this sunless sunset.

through the edges of miracle can i imitate my own sorrow? someone is waiting for me on a bench holding yellow candles in her hand.

the bench floats in a battlefield. the föhn blows in pictures of southern clarity. she helps me plant fennel along the asymptotes towards infinity.

we will meet again at the depression into which the moon has fallen. will cover the cracks with a cloth woven from the frustration in our dreams.

we will throw a subtle veil of violet over the petrified refusals.

i want to reassure you about my attempt to build walls bodies can walk through. wade with me into the shallows of an unsteady welcome. a rusty anchor has caught onto the experiment. hold on to my tachycardia. you didn't think the water would be this cold or this clear?

Before World War II, the St. Gallen chief of police Paul Grüninger (1891–1972) saved the lives of several hundred Austrian Jews fleeing the Nazi terror. He risked his career as a policeman in doing so, enabling them to enter legally into Switzerland by falsifying the entry dates on their documents and circumventing the edicts sent out by the authori-

ties in Bern ordering those controlling the borders to refuse admittance to Jewish emigrants. When his superiors discovered that Grüninger was disobeying orders, the chief of police was suspended from his duties, and then dismissed, and charges were laid against him for the falsification of official documents. Paul Grüninger was not fully rehabilitated by his canton and country until the mid-1990s.

domitilla: returning through the deleted door

Tillemont says that among the martyrs in the persecution of Domitian none are more illustrious than his nearest relations — Clement his cousin-german and the two Domitillas, wife and niece of Clement. Some persons, much impressed with the multiplication of the saints and martyrs, have supposed that there was only one Saint Flavia Domit-illa, and that the discrepancies in the account of her relationship with the Emperor, and the probable mistakes made in copying from the manuscripts the name of the island to which she was banished, which is given by some writers as Pontia and by others as Pandataria, led to the supposition that there were two. . . . it is, however, not the least unlikely that there were two Domitillas, aunt and niece.

there was a certain competition for good places, near martyrs † a draught of brightness slips in † a canary friend exults † the range of transformations escapes the situation of a model biographer † to separate not with regret nor evenly stitch acceptance to loss of the substituted less

shows the abodes of the living and dead in close contiguity † what the antique stores † apertures † passages of serious above pass through illegible loopholes † the underground capitulates to excavations as unaccompanied on sunday after taking wine in the kitchen glides to an inveterate gossip

a city beneath the earth . . . an inexhaustible supply of relics † jour-neys end in the unseen passages of another's roots † perfectly disordered intricates lecture for a worn-out immediately † as the nearest dream recedes others beyond scrutiny rear out of customs at minority sites † lorries with summer tyres carry the crust from that direction

IN PACE † in the same place a mouthway bashfully spaces † narratives frighten with the reverse of † edged with flowers and folly they revive a lost solicitude attired and filled with transferables

† far from heaven as the rest travel first class slowly puts forth †
leaves their

difficult always to assign meanings appropriate to death † and to
perpetuate this day's journey from the absolute † by arguing
for marks that begin from reciprocal † unbecoming the hidden
adventures binding to tend us † where we wear time where we
meet our desires counterfoil

boxes of books appear over and over again † they move † the spirits
ask us there they raise our disguises † the ordinary looks sleepily
at the residue fixed to collared orders † waiting for us to welcome
us they welcome each other † earliness peaks

*perhaps the pictures indicate that in certain circles relations between
adherents of the old and new religions were far more friendly than our
literary sources admit* † their advice between the two leave me leave
you with conjectures † nights without similarity communicate
what we understand † spirits from new prophecies in another
world gather to the naive † at supper we learn to laugh again to
engage in meeting the cold

others in the catacombs † remember quelling the continuity † but a
sunset on the dawn of reason offers no alleviation † work towards
horizons of thinking no † rashly but overwhelms me † so the
treasure bears a resemblance to contain

*No convincing evidence exists for a Domitianic persecution of the
Christians. The growth of the legend may well be impressive, but the
consistent development only serves to weaken the case, as must hap-
pen when Flavius Clement's wife (and mother of his seven children)
is transformed into his virginal niece and claimed as one of the first
virgin martyrs.*

julian: dance for three voices

scene: a town screened by walls out of focus far away. some hand writing thereabouts.

enter elena wounded and stricken.

elena: i withdraw from bruised and swollen flesh an arrow. i amuse myself with nemesis. my steps continuously return to something violent. things said.

myself enters resolute and gentle.

me: wait before you acquiesce to particularly. we have enough parts here to go back into preoccupations. *(in an undertone)* then with the unrecognized the next wish moves to the centre.

enter julian wearing on the third finger a ring of tricks.

julian: i too conceive a mighty desire to receive three wounds in my life: the wound of very contrition   the wound of kind compassion   and the wound of wilful longing.

me: so. i. no. modify the tellings. examine the back of me. speak against a world of whispers. because suffering shines and memories of everything negate the delicate.

we proceed. we play with the atrocious and marvellous on a lake that fertilizes and engulfs over the property. we stroke every hair deprived of consolation. we turn we enter a system of sufficient.

me: toleration takes up the plot bestowed and introduces aversion. quite certain of a first performance.

exit elena and julian. thunder. the smell of burning flesh.

me: *(improvising)* my mouth has one border along meanings. a footpath diffuses through situations crossing in front of extraordinary echoes with the reverberation of retreats. abandons the glittering so much. sweet hearts begin to take care of yourselves.

you enters.

you: you ruin more. in a word: prejudice. producing disasters cheerfully. *(sighs.)* a trifling twist of before. *(shudders.)* undefiled. no. crushing to pleased. weary teasing. no fate produces nothing. no love. no probable. the wicked covet contagion and you they hold warmly.

me: vehemently.

you: in a nearness where fingers hiss. moisture gives orders. hard caresses a thigh.

me: come in. your fingers can lightly test these articles. you have the strength to judge your submission. hatred cannot consume its loathing or slake its thirst on a developing love. loathing the dreadful claws. nothing communicates through the speeches of the dead. as my strongest point kills love stirs. i owe to you.

exit you and me. a long pause.

● ● ●

scene: open. some small forms in the faults to arouse curiosity. a jet of geometric water glints strangely. it rescues the sleeping. the jet indeed watches.

refreshed myself enters.

me: facts succeed when their meanings feel inclusive. and so the music we suffer imprisons us in a house of performances.

after a few moments elena enters awkwardly.

elena: i do not go yet. i must have time to remember. perpetually speaking until a result. i range through madness through intervals of calm disgust to this quarrel.

you enters. faces the air. thinks over the breaks. speaks.

you: nothing new please that does not also take care for essential customs. no narratives might perforate time. always writing to have. to possess.

enter a doctor who moves sideways.

doctor: thigh haunch leg limb
knee kneecap peg pin
cut it down   cut it out   cut it off
for a first-class performance

doctor exits choosing the remote. silence. a fallen hand on the ground speaks.

hand: come in. the view pleases. your infinite rises and slips.

elena and a shadow cross the beach.

you: with what intensity. with what longing. do you not understand the ecstasy which senses may reach and apprehend.

a weight larger than love. a moment heavier than desire. pavements inside.

elena: i lie on the salt grass though my hands may never guide their guilt to pierce ionospheres.

me and you leave. a remarkably beautiful figure waits listening to these appetites. susana enters in mourning.

susana: i cannot write a beautiful story with a beginning and an end from what i know.

susana stands up offering an empty space to and greeting julian.

susana: rubies. so dark. glowing.

elena: we follow tracks in the sand.

julian: i have teachings within me. the beginnings of an a b c.

elena: i remember a child that stares at a stranger and the child's name.

julian: rods and scourges. thorns and nails. drawings and draggings.

susana: see how the bees fly carrying yellow.

elena: how can we ever know

julian: dreadfully clothed

elena: if we walk through the doors of gold and silver.

susana fetches an amber bead. a large heavy bead of thick cloudy yellow. the last bead from a broken necklace.

elena: my mind goes over the problem.

julian: with all our hearts   with all our souls   with all our mights

elena: i tremble. i feel the same.

julian: and thus we have matter of mourning. and we have lasting matter of joy.

they embrace. susana wanders in sleep through the space. even elena cannot reveal the innermost key or the clue to the rest of the mystery.

susana: you do not know what you want.

a splash of light. susana kisses elena with her soul. exeunt.

●   ●   ●

scene: a corpse in petticoats works at a machine. with no one else on the stage it kicks rhythmically watching the ghost of susana.

enter julian.

julian: and these two parts in me: susana and elena. but one soul. so susana ever in peace with listening in full joy and bliss. and elena — sensuality — suffers for the salvation of speaking. and these two parts i see and feel in a deviant showing in which my body fills with the feeling and mind of elena's passion and susana's dying. and furthermore with this subtle feeling and a secret inward sight of the absent parts. they arrive in the same time.

time: the present. a sonorous footstep reflects its walk. the corpse hits upon a device. it sleeps. it has a face full of knowledge. a face. a clock stops. the mind grows up in impressions seduced by the real provoked by the suggestion that if you drop the conditions for this travesty runs on violence along a street of wounds where every neighbour entices you into a caress of closeness you perform. no not me but a slight youngster with a harp enters from the west. this certain person weeps. o kiss me. so kiss the corpse the pallid one on the move. howl and kiss. this road for living persons and lunatics turns. then painfully the corpse in pantaloons lends you the hand. you need not only courage for this street but a wine-red imagination.

julian: soon all closes.

hand: take pleasure in.

corpse: in sensible. in animate. in the centre of a dead body.

the hand slips within my breast.

julian: and that by the gracious touching of sweet lightening of ghostly life whereby we keep in true faith hope and charity with contrition and devotion and also with contemplation and all manner of true joys and sweet comforts.

we wake. we wake slowly under yellow clouds.

caterina: a generic letter

dearest. my essence shivers. my impure and eloquent blood approaches grief. apprehends again in the end of a century of *careful education. early aspirations to become a nun frustrated by relatives.* issues loop their anchors into me. why delves. delights in writing no stranger to more. invents until *her parents married her to giuliano adorno.* understanding dissolves in reflections formulating clues *during an unhappy political marriage.* from late questions to although gravity reaches the depths of well necessitating qualifications. and under the surface suffering the names of marvels *she was converted by a mystical experience.* much surrenders to the depths of well. woe falls into the conditional mood. potable but not essentially. *for twenty-three years she was unable to eat during lent.* negatives leaner than the irrational. a patience so distinctly eroded emerging from the depths of well *she felt stronger than when she ate.* in the depths of well what compassion engorges glistening parodies to foster reunion with the same. *with assiduous service to the poor and sick.* so much beauty actually leaks. empties. every day death disregards children's innocence and the records seem only to invite sentences adjusted to agree with my recognizing the sense in her body thought universes. efficiently. *in a hospital she was administrative head from 1490 to 1496.* not the last experiment in quelling what. scents of lavish gardens. secrets of gracious confidences. the *"trattato del purgatorio" and the "dialogo" are spiritual classics.* backwardly humans even accepting the bottom of well delete speech. *her authorship has been denied.* their. frequently. bottom of well. love.

galswintha: in the school for anger

vehicle for dispensing with in facts — *daughter of athanagild king of the visigoths* in those days of duality — historical thistles distaff flight from the reprimands of separation — a fog of livid identities hangs over the water — changing reticence into having desire — resenting an *infinite number of wives* — and because the nearest dismays perilous nettles force a way into the account — *the former ones were put away* bewildered — or not —

the manner in which a dead acerbity has to make me feel extremely uncomfortable — or the ill humours that seam normality — the reason why *was induced* sluggishly — indignity meets a cup of coffee — an african success — no feigning the growing enmity of opinions to the revelations — the clandestine sarcasm of death acquaints us with a lack of curiosity degrades — hug the knows — *the king received her with an immense dowry in gold and jewels* — to dam the pleasant — untie a constant exasperation scrupulously setting down this one without sole rights — the stammerings of subtracted solutions in a discourse abrade one into promptly devising moments of impatience in the life of *Galswintha's mother Goiswintha* — in flowing to possess unhappiness irascible tasks sore one's consent to the benefits — so much to call up improvise continually be afraid and alarmed as they *stood in a half circle and swore fidelity to her as to a king* recklessly — lashed to an attempt — terse — threatening when abandoning — a curfew on irritation otherwise — *she was not beautiful* — and we shall not haughtily forget — eat *gentleness and tact* whosoever it may intolerate — forced into the party with inconsistent unwillingness stains *several others to make way for* — and not only poetically and rhetorically ire cautiously delights the soul if everyone hosts thoughts to make amends for oversights walled up in abridged — we have to run through so many layers — through the loess of years *aware in due time* — and the carmine explosion of mere convictions — lasting indignity with myself roused to harbour alarm — grimaces stick to the concealed me — resolute to show furious — *our heroine requested that he would send her back to her own country — offering as the price of her liberty to leave him all her dowry* — how determination composes the tools to process death — some indulgence please for storms relieve the unattractive dangerous subjects — perhaps — by reforming the representations a great quantity of heat that anybody or somebody remembers — ducts — *but very soon afterward she was strangled in her bed by one of the king's pages* —

thrusts daily — when incomprehension has *penetrated deep into the stone floor* of old closed conversations cannot divert — a carefully dressed austerity signifies studying defended snatched moments lift the covers to reach another's worn habit of wisdom — *other miracles followed* — as they recede the covers unattach — wanting slackens — a frugal supper simmers courage entitled to myselves carefully plural — *although her worship does not appear to have been sanctioned throughout* —

the king married fredegonda —

withouts rejoin to arrive at the conclusion *brunehault probably had a deep affection for her gentler sister* — these the pearls ourselves — *that her sister's position and life should be sacrificed for any woman was unpardonable* — the documents leap to stun every move towards farewell — in the flash of complaints a good amount needs amending — hoards move with kindred creatures in the same embroiled medium suffocates —

start again —

heartsharp —

very dry remarking —

tense —

maria maddelena de'pazzi: return to a sanguine account

in an effort to moderate the space of more —
                    the humiliations of a mongrel intellect discovers
bleached knotted into a colourless bias —
                    where returning to the deletions
in exhausted journeys into being reconstructs the neverblossoms of
a later may —
                                        on the most renovated day
of the week — the day of release — when soothe rolls up with
suffering —

                    each childhood seduced in pain
dies like the illumination in moderately — on a beach enclosed by
errors and stairs the mysteries of deep-blue kindnesses release their
dented voices with the levity of improvidence —

                                        fast words words of
the infinite corpuscles —
                    repeat — repeat — the moments when gestures
transformed the gaze into a breeze —
                                        and oh if plants could love
and clouds could open and could the unabandoned — an
accidental mystery burnishing skin to the aspirated page —
                    dregs of beginning chewed into a lapse in
time and each sense settles into confrontation without end —

plastic covers the dung like print the handwriting —

            a pure photograph of every year —

                                    out of the unavailable epistemology
of introverts neither has the babble disappeared —
                    a lettered view where less has visited the next stanza —
                                    a name in a pocket of choices like

water in a broken calabash —

      baking a cake with the flour of angels and the butter of
queens —

delight possesses where the deity disappears —

      the coming issues maybe —
            me in the meeting —
               good dressed in a fraction
of abandon —

                          entreaty
as the mother of distance —

risking to create in the losses and robberies of variety —

      aspiring to the mystery of the word the monster of
desire exhibits a perception of the word as the liberated other expir-
ing in their exchange —

                        come my
dove —

come my eagle —

      come my pelican — symbols of invention in the
soul —

                    mad in the
matter of the mother —

sorrow rides through the loops of devastated sights — the sister's
idea appears like a gesture without the revised version —

      how to relate the marks flow through the pass of
reality —

                    the marks
with the mass and the mess of life —

      just as the red in the sea leaks into the provinces of captivity diversity lies buried in the tombs of the heart —

silence sickens with concern —

on the dusty road to death of one
some children play to win with marbles the colour of menstrual
blood and the eucharistic egg —

a sky of mysterious words
clouded by even more mysterious images aposemantic sym-
bols meaningless formulations descriptions of a trialled
life —

the transcription of muteness
into a field of inconsistency

jeanne: requisitioned voices

24 february 1431

> *Asked whether it is an angel of God, without intermediary, or the voice of saints, she responded that it comes from God. "And I believe that I am not telling you fully every thing that I know; And I am more afraid of saying something that will displease them, than I am of answering you."*

*   *   *

place: shrine of notre-dame de bermont in lorraine on the hill just above a holy spring.

time: 30 may 1426

voice 1: pity will fill the occasion with a score for late tambourines. i after the passion.

jeanne: needing verbs to ask the birds into a circle. what occasion? i only ask you or they will scold me to tame.

voice 1: a rigorous heart to guard identity. a creature alone. a species of impotent eloquence.

voice 2: what you will send into the flooding river of night. when all of nature's alleyways empty.

jeanne: they nag me when i come here. their questions haunt me like hungry ticks seeking skin to sink their teeth into.

voice 2: i will give you a ring rarer than zinc to wear on your sixth finger. it will protect you from the corrosion of rage more than silver can or an eye of lapis lazuli. the ergot in the chaff will heal the child inside denied entry to a cold house without windows or doors.

voice 1: and i will help you define it in the invaginated generosity of silence.

voice 2: scratch my academic cheek and it will bleed for you. oval and uncut numbers in the ominous operas of mankind.

jeanne: i kiss that cheek. but the letters taste of a numbness i cannot learn or laugh at.

voice 2: jeanne do not tire in the interrogation. an alto reaches the highest octaves of cloud.

voice 1: on the stroke of logic a reason will cheat you of vitality.

voice 2: under a kindled touch you will find our iterations.

voice 1: all the answers spiralling through the accounts as if their cinders could choke their erosion. they will scan you from the nape of ignorance into the digital echoes of their own.

voice 2: economical with arguments that turn on a trust. come jeanne the documents grow like azaleas on a dry soil one by one their stems rushing into a miracle (or a mirage) of nattering arguments — pink white and blue.

voice 1: we provide you with tutelage in the real.

jeanne: i come you say incidental to a modern plot?

voice 2: your credentials will raise the chimes to the highest pitch of matter. persist in offering them outrages in a certified mail. addressee not known.

voice 1: not pessimistic otherwise your ears will hear etched into the ether superstitious zones of an inky madness. oneiric and abandoned.

jeanne: you want me to lead a troop of pages against a fence of eglantine? to cross a delta of laughter into a crescent of rogues.

voice 2: perhaps a circle of lark's eggs served in a fancy title. lent-en. but not lenient.

jeanne: i see a street of tears and melting tar. i smell corpses whose bones obey the salt.

voice 2: these pictures to colour with the undertones of monody.

jeanne: you say i will ride like the ancients into a noble account my answers will always torch?

voice 2: as illegitimate as manners gilded in belief.

jeanne: the proof is like a tuber dormant in zeal? a conscience that cannot choose the ends it will serve?

voice 2: quasi fine.

jeanne: until an angel of.

voice 1: not to fall from the earth when the princes of ipse dixit swallow you into the smoke of otiose cigars to cure their impotence with the zapped virginity of an innocence they lost in italics.

jeanne: you deluge me with labours like the anagrams of a fel-ony.

voice 1: obliterate the need. your heart lies in easeless sapwood. invocate us as enzymes in a reaction of furious virtue. soldiers will sell your past.

voice 2: like a peg burning in a vast hole of oil. your disgrace will zigzag between the eminent in other words. in the powdered orrisroot they discover the incense called lament. just one item in a zone of icons impalpable but imbued with the lipid extras of an unavailable saint.

jeanne: i feel like a pirate. a scandal or an interval that lives only to march into others' orders.

voice 2: let them bathe you in their absurdities.

voice 1: you will amaze them like a mazzard blossoming in snow.

jeanne: i want to suck the marrow of cosmic openings. but a cadaver of ice has fallen over them.

voice 2: bask in doubts as you like through to a parisology. i will venture to intervene in the fifth quadrant on the palm side of the lisp. a civet cat brought me a solution to survive. i lost my panic on night rides.

jeanne: and as i get nearer to the task?

voice 2: each version will open poised with a cross in its tale.

voice 1: and the net will be tatted with the eyes of preying mantises. the dead will cry for you.

voice 2: venerate the dictates of your reason. don whatever solutions you need to evade the units of molar men.

voice 1: a resistance in the notional.

voice 2: or couched in terms that chide us to offer a quandary of costs the enigmas can never balance.

jeanne: i cut a vein yesterday — cautiously — and my choices congealed to the odour of acceptance. then the ants came to take away the good from me.

voice 1: a steady chorus of chills. from death to a voracious design remembering the moments a person pierces what the angles evoke.

voice 2: gusts of interpretation will clutch at you. you will turn on the rack of their caprice until the cicatrice is what you are.

jeanne: and on those terms you say i will be culled for infinity or until another one charms them with her innocent arrogance of form.

voice 2: home when you come to where the nouns no longer flee under force their niches of illegality.

jeanne: and will you send me a dove as silent companion into that terrible zone of azure fevers and nausea?

voice 1: fear not jeanne. they will copy you. they will copy you into the urchin of a land or a universe of tangents.

jeanne: don't inform me. far away gliding on an island of ul-tramarine tests. soon i will quit this ditty for a nemesis you cannot escape me from.

*   *   *

27 february 1431
> *Asked whether it was the voice of angels or saints or of God without intermediary, she replied that it was the voice of Saint Catherine and Saint Margaret. "And their forms are crowned with beautiful crowns, with rich and precious ornaments."*

modwenna: fragment from a neglected life

for jocelyn wogan-browne

1   like silver needing polish,
cracks the cement they perish,
a child a name to cherish,
to curl into its soft dish.

2   had eve found this nunnery
would she have jumped jittery
out of her green frippery
into its deep damask drapery?

3   not to restore a nature,
to fête or fudge a figure
charred by receipt until pure
contaminates this our scripture.

4   when we devised needle and pen,
when we teach moons to the children
of star-eyed barren women,
when our wounded dances waken

5   the judges from tombs of envy,
we've been condemned to heavy
sentences but masks of ivy
hide our lemon smiles and savvy

6   eyes. recall our aunts who fought
to distil and save each thought
etiolating through what was taught
into the breach of sun it sought.

7   take a peach, a hand, a poise,
cut flesh to the stone of noise
as blue as eve's mouth, as the turquoise
pitted with sound and flawed joys.

8   at dawn i rise and count the spiders
whose webs embroider spare covers
for our dreaming books. their powers
in dust like angelic fevers.

9   and as the apostrophe rends
the owner from his possessions, friends
send me messages whose silence bends
round my veiled welcome to broken ends.

10   we have no keyholes in our doors
that we have carved with minotaurs
and shine with milk that pours
from mothers' rocky breasts. whose sores

11   remind us just how far desire
must fall through certainty. wire
frames support grief until we tire
of the weight of our repertoire.

12   the queer distraint of our folly:
as if will and the courtly
charm of hybrid tastes were likely
to poison nature with nearly.

13 nature! different each day
    and the same, its mean laws lay
    out curves that plunge into play
    with our hair on pillows of hay.

14 and they asked me what the pig meant
    when it explained it had been sent
    to eat trifles and collect the rent
    they lost their fear in the moment.

15 grind some basil, a leaf of mint,
    wrap them in a circle of damaged lint
    with powdered sulphur and a hint
    of honeydew. when the spirits squint,

16 swallow it. as vice melts we hear
    the wedged voices that drink each tear
    as if the salt they bring could sear
    an old script into the new year.

17 our tunes wax and wane, lunar
    patterns pulled from the sun's grammar;
    each poor word opens her vulva
    touched by a marigold flower.

18 modwenna resurrected

    [the remainder of the manuscript has been lost]

lutgard: it is time for many variations

version d
excited too by what we dread.

in constant prayers and fasts for 14 years she offers up her condition
to appease the anger of heaven. simplicity as contemporary as this
sketch for an unpredictable doubt. fascicles bound in red leaves for
the ultimate lecture.

what's left behind instructs on various ways to cherish and imag-
ine that as the florid suitor tries to carry her off by force her spine
cracks from grammatical identity.

without delay dissolve the story reflects her interpolation and as
she dies at the end of her third fast of seven years her generosity is
feminine.

version b
and always anchored in hesitations.

the money intended for her marriage portion lost in business
speculation lavishes a nation of credulous competitors. she describes
them by departing for an unknown language where she fastens
onto soul-fed facts.

the legacies she speaks dry in the sun of her cheek and as she creates
her cosmos of indications fiery drops of blood dismay her forehead
and hair. cramps attach the very self that cancels the correction of
it.

eleven years before her immediate death her eyes turn liquid and
she loses sight of the raconteur. accepting this affection with a rig-
orous joy she studies the comings and comings in the hearts of
women.

version c
eventually too reckless.

laughter might sacredly wound the state of ignorance. attractive simultaneous describes and divides. on a frivolous visit to those sealed facts may sully the conversation of love.

as she levitates from the ground with a halo of letters around her head divinity cheats on her constructions rationing and rostering the body of her knowledge — crammed a tide into a tic. a star into a steroid.

drawn into the stricter convent of the instant of the unstable report of the reflexive reading how courage flees the defined.

sexburga: imaginary letters in translation

because we are the daughters of king anna we will endow a place in a tradition of incorruptible endings.

jeopardize the scene with our bones. around these tied tombs they will edit our lives unconsumed by the spaces in time.

shrewd. and emotional. a male socially. scandalous family of patronage.

i see the fens hung with your portrait in the moon. i sing a mass of blood-stained letters. i value this continent of flesh.

they need structures to bury the dead and wall us in alive. on sundays they preach and prance trading in our illicit relics. our alimony of compromise. one day ladies with trousseaus of breeches and cancellous canes will form an academy of laughter to put the ribs back to back into fashion.

i bequeath you my daughter eormenilda a riddle of extravagance and through your daughter werberga we will consummate these elite constructions and they will call us saints.

let the future decide whether this is love legal or seditious. we dreamed in faded focus.

that the spirits of your friends — the dadaists the debaters the demythologizers — interpellate the seems of your immersed body with a fertilizing scatology.

like a dulcimer exposed to speculations your decomposed voice reaches me through charred leaves each article an inaudible flower in the lesson.

you left me to leaf through me with the sharp dagger of your motives enter the arteries to my heart. they build machines to melt the sky but rare soft silver-white our familiars petrify the fire.

famished recognition if i call you ishmael or the magic sickness that we share.

in poems stratified like water i can almost feel the date. the cold. they found my words plaited in your sighing hair. i took the ring moulded on your finger. i drowned into two blue moons. indigenous eyes. they have no pupils. only delphiniums leaping from death's fog against the light.

if i have the perseverance to follow through your severe imagination will you release me from a sister's solitude?

you slumber in the possible. your delicate letters seep like blood through the drama of masked men. we fasten through this day on the grammars of the dead.

the dangers of love you say to me. traded for the conclusion of ideas. the seamy secrets in scriptures.

risking a performance of embodied incompletion : a siamese edition : an incursive flow.

the finesse of your excitement like an accident in femaleness. scarring the social. healing them with sharpened breath. questioning the deficiencies where we famished our relatives in incestuous orders.

my feminism : lips just hold the names maintain the material man-ifestations. a trail and a trial of silk syllables stretched across the silent curves of mathematics.

streets filled with the noise of tears. i tried to touch the pronouns to trace the crime that floods the dream like cream in the devil's coffee. i heard my fortune in the very moment her heart misses a beat. on any corner of any modern city where the beggars mend our speech.

allusive speech. folded like our labia. permeated by your salt-stained breath a theory of continuous origins.

cautious because a latent delight could leave the scene when we open our eyes to the fantastic mistake called attraction.

dear e.,

errors as tic(k)s. how we inherit our mitochondria. definitely no one imagined (at least) two as she pumped adrenalin into our f(r)ictional hands.

in a room in the tate gallery a view with a text and the sense that distance comes in the colours we eat the unnatural ones the tin(t)s in our curses.

if at the end o-motions anticipating the antics in the antique. how i came to mash chillies into your body and spread butter along the nerves of a race we never lost.

my forms follow reading yours (appear to) follow mine. **bold.** a self-maroon(ed) collective.

straight out fudging the zones. delinquent labour past bows and invitations delving into the (w)holes and the reccage. in another words trance and chance well met in lower casements. alice does now. on the bend at the modern end of the longest river in history : Δ : a tract for diverging outlets and a symbol of omission.

let's sin : writing. magmatic folios or maybe computer screens (screams) for e(cstatic)-femails. creatures my sweet sweat passes (out) to the mahogany.

all that energy condensed in granite. delirious near the end i send you perhaps a phrase in egyptian (a lovefable. a tendril of providence).

yours,

g.

isabel: the cost of assurances

shady walks as surf. a small orchestra
beats the writing table and old demons follow
elite curves. bliss while caryatids demolish
what stays. anyone can unexasperated by
recommend arriving slowly. light-intentioned
lucifer dreams concisely. explosions
of waiting. comb through who through
the locks glimpse strife when
ever enters into collisions of exchange.
laughter betweens me as someone washes over
the etched kisses. existence pronounces
ill at ease without my whines. and fetid
remains convulsed with ill consider how blowing
may remedy atrocities dwell. a boding

from all parts of Europe referred their differences to her

consecrates a moment: "acceptance because trust
me and associate me with mother"
as prelude to recounting how stimulated
by contrasts come together rich. a quarter
of good to gather ill favours sharing
who trusts ebullience erupts. forced to ex-
acerbate the good-ill of pidgin
whole these needy people situated in much.
spasms of whether. by now at last goes
disappears into unacceptable
a generation can knock down dynasties. but
the old remember. arrest information.
name the request. in hospitable eraises
a year of dislocations and learn to quake
remedies my moves swiftly and suddenly
perishes. amber-coloured liquids separate
when from ever sickens. how not to forget
debates. words reach adjust

voluntarily gave up part of her

unbalance. falling obliged to break out
of essential. autoburst. errors have moments
of sarcasm too. have. my bubbles to flow and
go deforms my. trials and explosions persevere
on all sides incline from cultures cannot allay
troubles. ill liberates fond. huge disappointments
emerge from competitions but do not shrink
from daily up to something a mess promises.
absorbing documents inexperience
depasses extremes but comes in on lines nearly.
think about during. spread out for triple the time
perhaps the time after words. might have turns
aside not amiss. allowances together
to a fault. hands bell. ours unseals smoothness de-
taches these recollect my takes and teachers.
fondled nonsense. an uncertain heart impulsed
to allow reaching beyond

regardless of the stones and arrows flying about her

regulations for public order. or
a psychoscape of embattled folds. or
the power to behold flat. through their entrances
murderers leave compelling undeceives
unaccounted for and unending. strangled
and enraged others edit what we have
concealed truths break. into before language.
shame exploded empty pours out through attack.
open contains terrified. extinctions.
tabernacles of flesh like unfamiliars
wear unanalysable forms copy a way
out neglecting the last minute comes and goes
in a giggle. a year signals efforts
to follow to an end ungrammatical
dynasties glide through stone shivers. the long point

of the noiseless consider turning aside
from effort robs this cause commits an offence as
soon as
                    dispatches you

Isabel de paz, the Mother of Peace

anne askew: diving into the night

first examination in the madness of reality. not to satisfy your expectations with eloquent lamentations and to. fine lines drawn into alternative rooms sealed in suppose. fine masses at every gate. is excused concerning that matter of charming cheats. erased directly in all things mingling the fallen causes in a civilized does it practise? confronted with a question the foreigner should answer the custommonger with the fare of bishoped accusations. to utter all grave speechlessness. utter to the bottom of the longest perforation impressed into cheerfulness. on the points of perhaps but how much. would not but concluded an era of ageing novelty. have said having said already that the hand of the clock has reached the accident.

now remember them the gifts of the cheapjacks and the cheated devils. an involuted desire to enter the darkest days until tantalized finally reach the rotten grapes. the conclusion perfused by unmortified perfumes of a corpse waving in a corked tunnel. come on come out the hanged cat will show you informed constellations. but for that later examination where these ailing lines crash obstinately into a brief drama in the flesh. that abominable godspell where the feat of suffering would have robbed even donald duck of his quackery. your highnesses the apostolic traitors. gentle men your lack of poetry amazes us. burdened by confessions we can only point out that the purpose of these jokes impregnates the disease cleanly. say gall hidden in a broken shell. by what type do you possess all the glee. say that the letter stays returning to its absolute performance anchored in a dissolving sense. for the heifer would not sing a new song to the lord until she had reached a stranger land. a parrot risks the pit of fossils. five hours continuous conversion of choked into charred.

deny it again. grilled for the material thing that very high ending intensified curve by curve meeting in a paradise of sky-green inconceivables. you forgets what to signify with. more complicated than any pattern a remembrance of spots. method dwells in nothing material. dive into the sudden silence with stony hearts around your necks. written.

we will waltz in deflected decisions will stumble into the audience will inter their essence in attitudes of vitality. condemned in secrets without a quest. o people of death. the only remedy fragiles customs. discord glistens in what would they need to know. a wafer collects the titular spores. the lamp on the table grows needy with the light. as a good memory although established its retails price as a persistent veneration of nervous visions.

the uniqueness unavailabled in the moment. presses its double against an unworthy average. poised at that well deceived neither by liberty nor a hollow consciousness. as conscious as the counter of guesses unfolding the vulvate.

smartly dressed in purple contradictions. on the rack. on the rack a very long time. lying in willed questions bitten by icicles and rats. internalize what the technicians can achieve. with a standard error of plus or minus please. leave my opinion transmits onto a wide empty screen of appearances. farewell dear friend and prey.

past excuses painted on the dry pavements of chronology. i have made a copy discreet in its honours personal in its promises. consign it to the water of trouble holding no opinions contrary to contrasts. and as i trust in the appearance of bravery plunge into the magnificent clutches of hermeneutic surgeons ungrazed by the sharp shingle that maims the eradicated age. where the idol admitted to the idyll laughs its incredible greed. each member standing in its deictic grace more macabre than what they wear. because the weak things of the world hide a mighty obstinacy. put on your props. give me into the notion of addled bones. of initials zipping up the atomic zones. and perhaps a conclusion of anxiety. done. she staked her feathers in the comedy and a dozen valkyries laid their larvae in the crime.

[anne askew's heart was accused of heresy maybe because of her diabolic denial of the supposed catholic doctrine of transubstantiation (dark to me) and long ritual of the mass. imagine according to her own account how her dull husband thomas kyme drove her from their allopathic household after she violated prohibitions against lady-fingered participation in theological debate and scriptural interpretation (part in memory). tormented governmental authorities in london then interrogated her in two maddened rounds that ended with the unprecedented application to a precious gentlewoman of the fully indecent rigour of torture and the glittering rack in an unsuccessful obscened attempt to force her to recant her posture. on 16 july 1546 during the certain closing months of henry viii's lamentable reign she burned socket and soul at the stake.]

margaret of antioch: a pregnancy

notwithstanding that you could not withstand the humours leaking through the holes in your hands. from your mortified pragmatics spring saturated mauves. the improbability of belonging to the ricochet too. to the numbers conceived and censored. in these displaces — moors of universal time spluttered with poppies. i came to zion to drink decay. to corinth to piss in sound holes with the prostitutes. the matter of the fact overflows the pot. before the noise can.

sign if if you can't in vitro. or with the sun and wind console a field of rice. then a delicate paper aquarius carried to restrain the alterations. closed in the vice of being. in glass-fronted cupboards (but dust finds the keyholes) on the anatomy room ceiling. you try to touch the physiognomy of the name. move in a hidden frame. outside is tense as you dance at a ball with disruptive abilities. isolation teaching you the alphabet.

and for the room where your nerves synapse with aluminium. a woulded hollow. broken windows on the rim of a circle of inborn errors of discrimination. delirious with diseases of multiplied indifference we collaborate in a shiver of now your mouth touches the alarm knots. from alpha to the scent of vanilla. i promise to put my irregular peg in a categorical hole. to lick your knowledge the catalyst in the pain. to confuse the shape ignores the urge excreted in the function.

through the poles through the dragon's mouth back to a bitten apple. the way in which comes to politics. and so she faces and effaces the company of her indicated other. scarred hands endorse the bone broken from her rocking back tracing the story of twinned days a prophet induced the words out of a saline symbiosis. and sent her back to solitude.

I, Margaret, also pray to you,
God, that you give me power
To protect any pregnant woman
If she crosses herself
With a book containing the story of my life,
Or opens it,
Or places it on her body,
So that she be granted a safe delivery.

margaret: and they call it the valley of passion

the salient dimensions of day slow. gold memories of an interior and a penumbra of thoughts alone. a night of real yellow. grey clouds without the dimensions of day quench your attention. you really don't know where your axes went on a voyage where characters switch points from a passed age. in the night you do the really deep mining. with hearts as intricate as personality mistakes pasted to the page. how can you not drink the terror of no retrievable mechanism. at the dim ends of the day holding a glass of thoughts looking inside into the dim reflections and fishy sentiments. while the next wave passes through you to the next line. sizing your day because you could not bear to live without memories. somewhere inside you write the shadows you think. a unique cord of interior characters scrambled in the crossing out. night. where the white tape ends and the dimensions of day knocking. your mother comes into the almost she cares for a lonely warmth. with eyes of a different hue seldom reaches her destination. her breath jewels her sweet weight on your heart her attention to parts. in the weak light she cultures a salty cordial troubled by no parallels. and in the night you can realize an angel blooming taller than day. you revere your mentor's paranoia. shakiness and interference on the sole of its sincerity you enter your personality. out paints the voyage. yes night the real lip of the crater your breadth your jaws dripping with rock thoughts. far inside the penalty of our species a thought scrambles up. into a pass lined with voyeurs and grey faces. you again really rather badly with eyes of a difference so expansive even day winces. you understand the interior as a dim idea with the soul and the heart thrown in. you understand the interior. but perhaps the sound of scars passing through. in the night you reel in the interludes exploring in a day of blue faces in your face. and perhaps the sound of grief in the rumour passages all grief. night truths. rules a bit rafferty. rubies bigger than apologies. the grace of death. if you could memorize every part and all their shadows. if you could memorize a single heart's corrosive detail. perhaps when your own stops in a bubble of air. but some nights you dance. sometimes in a black satin bow. sometimes in a narrow ribbon of yellow. then you have the dimensions of a storm whose feet may pass crazy to the centre. and that way you may scramble through. until one day the real fictitious word enters the opaque body. a word so alone and so sincere it infiltrates every character before the mistake can get crossed out. night. realized terrible and continuous.

mary magdalene: east of express

for certainly these teachings are strange ideas

a trace shows behind a lacquered screen. elegant T stretches into afterwords but characters turn away from wandering fine. T marks by wearing black lace before scattering to the bathroom. july sickens. a distant starved body spurns this scratching. an indication of old as yet unknown to possibility. into the bedroom a sour form leaves. at a quarter past the melody T asks for a photograph. softness consents to a composition thinly indulgent. through the echoes of dimness T draws a fabric of recollections. disclosures live in the aversions encounter arguments from one who interpretation pretexts. occasioned T abandons condolences wrapped in a semi-transparent shawl.

where the mind is, there is the treasure

coffee percolates. from the balcony a view of dreaming gestures. in C's hand twenty-nine pencilled messages to set the breakfast table in different positions. a catharsis of so much. childhoods of strict here comes today. except that to liberate suppose C first forms a delicate treat. from a moment of routine steals a buttered impulse. the milk jug holds treasuries. C spreads a dream of success on a slice of white change. the body sited melts into C's gaze. past time to the silences on dirty napkins. at a word works. casting the crumbs of morning. your opens a hope. making a shopping list of flying spices C puts damask to flesh and leaves to select finishes.

my mind between the two sees the vision

anticipate reaching out. draw the blinds down. champagne. a plate of daisies to gain or be undone. S arrives into a second of uncertainty. moist cheeks to conquer and a sealed book. orange silk skirts sophistication. through a small window a fine line of northern light crosses the unorthodox. puts a mattered to stereotypes in animated and forgotten confusions. on the pale bed cheek against an atmosphere of expectation S wears a glove of old delphic satin. S. an angular figure composing in distress seeking a sanctuary to preserve the unattainable precision. in the immediate discourse of compulsion S notices the shadow of life alone. a last lamina of excitement. to satisfy no more S departs. for cannelloni stuffed with particulars.

what binds me has been slain

to teach away petrified awareness. summer punch and a bowl of strawberries for M who requires every penny earned for a journey into tender. as success perishes with the overheated millennium directions become known. M talks about the reverse of arrives at esoteric stories. needs exclusion perhaps. has come to consider with alarm an environment growing old. overworked M stroking the lean grey pussycat. thus far ruled by opinions and domestication. M wants something to look for. a child with a gnawing sixth sense. a muscle-weary shaman. M who will go a separate way leans back from the slatted table. a supernatural butterfly reconnoitres empty glasses. M dozes on a tract between providers. renounces a biology of destroyed derivatives.

in a world I was released from a world

B's youth untraces. neglected by good breeding suffocates again. in a restaurant of difficult decisions B joins together insolvent conjectures. so a little laughter on the menu tonight. a sprinkling out of some secrets. a posture of self-respect worn until overdrawn. lapses. too much and not enough talking. the pianist plays a long absence. on the matter of lack B disapproves of crippled sentences. the pianist possibly on an impulse plays the tempos of the familiar passes. the wine comes from a village that trades honestly. a breeze leaves a privilege allowed to leak. B knows how to assault the reasons may keep their frenzy follows. B wants to dance. reaches for the vagabond. B's breast in front of.

do you think that I thought this up myself in my heart

perilously I sits on the edge of admission. perturbed. I's most seri-
ous possession. and perplexed. while the seventh demon waits out-
side

to proclaim and to preach
the gospel
according to
mary

faith hope and charity play poker at the end of the 21st century

faith hope and charity consent to a recording of their conversation during their annual outing to naming — its refuges and refusals.

faith: *(to us)* since the sixteenth century i have been told that verification is content without me. well today we invite you to join us to happenstance to leaky questions to a fresh delight on the cards. *(to hope and charity)* my deal i believe.

hope: i come from the fiery depths of sorrow. but first — greetings. to a day of differential intimacy and intimations of wisdom.

charity: in uncertainty. how to adapt the viciousness in uncertainty. how to appropriate the situation to where we meet. two cards please.

faith: i'll fold.

hope: can we never anticipate to hold the grief of all? i'll fold too. *(gathers up the cards)*

charity: well i would have lost that hand. i could not fill the gaps between ten benign rich and a queenly poor that constitutes my name. but the possible returns in a sincere revolt to unlimit the present. two again please.

faith: at night i climb ladders with rungs of sadness and antiphonies. three please.

hope: i'll not discard my lonely bursting heart. begin but never better.

charity: i fall into patience.

satisfaction in a game of poker. faith bets on piety and antonyms. delicate hope wins on sheer suspicion. summons toughness to another pair: dwelling and enduring.

faith: a prudent opening. three please.

hope: pass. my hand lacks precision because i never feel at home. capitalism excites my wrath. reason subjects me to.

charity: i cannot hold back millions until much more has departed.

some angels bring in a tray of virginal realities. faith nibbles a salty grace.

faith: i cannot move mountains with this pair.

hope: and i'll hand in good with desires.

charity: for those without hunger can easily gamble with death.

hope: i'll banish one.

charity: you play with the idea condemns us to difficulties. with the soured fortunes of benevolence. two please.

faith: the arrogant blossoms in unquestioning constancy. under the weight of soubriquets my mother carried a feather. much madness is diviner sense. and love chains us to consequence. again and again. i can do less with this hand.

hope sips a glass of spirit. decides that to bluff on a low pair of two sexes would not do justice to the point. shuffles and deals a new hand.

charity: keeping this hand i might perpetuate poverty.

faith: you must look inside to see whether you have meditation. three please.

hope: the fainter the more threatening. i'll also take three.

faith: beyond a doubt i'll bet you a prayer and a virtue.

hope plays on motivated by the exclusion of every possibility. faith misjudges.

faith: one old proposition and a new to perceive you.

hope: *(wearing an expression of silver)* excuse me from the next hand i need to go to the bathroom.

charity: we can wait until you get back.

hope: don't. unless i rush headlong into an accident.

faith: you won't.

during hope's absence faith and charity make a list of miracles to discuss after the salad lunch faith prepares with leftovers and some discreet nonsense. charity tramps around the kitchen in clogs.

*   *   *

faith: i have to bet until my last cent. *(drinks from a glass of water and unfolds a rather strong hand)* one card please.

hope: i'll disappear in this difference.

charity: some dark powers condemn us to justification. i won't take any cards.

faith conscious of possibilities bets cautiously but charity has a model based not on mystical language alone but also on deeds. faith's head bends to whatever shall appear. and gasps with hope as charity weakly reveals the royal flush she had dealt herself. faith mixes the cards well. you never know.

hope: you live through it day in day out. three please.

charity: the degradation of now lies in front of me. two please.

faith: if we destroy all models. the exception reforms me. i confess my ignorance concerning the sun the moon and the stars. what sort of bodies do genders have? it seems to me that time wears rags. i do not want to lose the lucidity of my trust. i'll take just one card.

hope: fifty parts. little by little. i have a fancy i shall probably replace some of my losses on these cards.

charity: *(wearily)* fold. *(looks out at the lake. and time.)* i must always adjust the borders.

faith: for the darkness of peace you can take this one hope.

charity:	open to the crimes of not giving. three please.
faith:	but i'll remember the sorrow of signs by folding.
hope:	i need something to drink. something clearer than the present. 150° proof. i'll also take three cards.
	faith leaves to work on this scale.
charity:	and will probably return with some ghastly fright we will have to sip line by line. i cannot stand the need for paper caution. i bet on my fury.
hope:	despite the need for caution i will raise you three blue skies.
charity:	nothing can forgive me my debts. a sugar island.
hope:	an attack by hope laments the same and feeds the fever. four silver linings.
charity:	i cannot stand without purpose. i need to see your hand.
hope:	*(laying down two queens)* these words have limited meanings for us to consider how we gamble with ourselves.
charity:	although old-fashioned ways no longer apply i give you my otherness. a slight answer. *(reveals three nines)*
hope:	there. never did quarrelling daughters lack a rash mother.
	faith returns with two gifts: a devout scarab for hope and understanding in a cage for charity.

charity:	*(somewhat fearful of provoking displeasure)* do you still want to play?
faith:	how else can the wind pass through obstinate hearts? three please.
hope:	*(to faith)* you don't look well. have you hurt yourself?
faith:	i have borne seven times. so perhaps you will laugh at my terror of learning my next lover has already died. the door keeps waiting for the perfection of an absolute future absent.
hope:	memory cheats us no less than the most profound discussions. three cards please charity.
charity:	you can sentence a sense but not without monstrous consequences. three for me too.
faith:	well i shall still weep dust and ashes. fold.
hope:	some artists devote their lives to building crushed statues. others conceal their truth in a chorus of plastic voices. charity you can take this hand.
faith:	really i don't want anything tangible but these conflicts in my breast . . .
hope:	oh give me a whisky and four cards. you sound as if you could make yourself without defects and deformities. do i play cards with you to look into my grave?
charity:	how can we play unmindful? one please.
faith:	performance by practice to effect a presence. i'll take

two.

hope: i cannot play without the noise of doubt.

charity: and i play not only to realize my limited capacities but to entertain rescue. i'll wager a magic carpet.

faith: i fancy a margherita. in all these extremes you mention i shall stand beside my own invention. a kiss. no. three kisses. you can not capture from me the confidences of death.

charity: the suffering side of my desires. you can take this purpose.

hope: maybe. however the longest day may close. perhaps release the noise hoarded in empty. how many charity?

charity: one for the good one for the bad and one for the bent in all people.

faith: one for excitement one for enthusiasm and one in spite of them.

hope: an immortal situation. i'll fold.

charity: our future still mistrusts those ready to alleviate the heartlessness of reason. shame may power my rage quibbles. i have files on total inadequacy. i support to signify. a finer earth mixes what it holds. i'll drop out.

faith: and to this we might add whatever else. the rift between humans and nettles. you cannot play poker alone. four please.

hope:	pass over the best into the relief of unfolding. two please.
charity:	i wonder about the remoter consequences. i'll take three.
faith:	not through some emotional disturbance i quit.
hope:	i ate a good breakfast. i'll wait for supper.
charity:	hope i sometimes think your confessions need to fit better. i'd like to see them.
hope:	don't intrude. i will sing nothing as the peak dissolves. i imagine the daily bread understood in a remade sense. two fives.
charity:	deliver me from waiting. a pair of jacks.
hope:	charity much as i love you and this game the unexpected infects the possible. three sixes.
charity:	ok. ok. i just want an open exchange. i suggest we bring this day to some kind of conclusion.
faith:	before you leave you must have something to eat.
hope:	i can stay for a few minutes.
charity:	me too. i have a passion for a bowl of greek yoghurt.
faith:	i believe i have some. and something to drink?
hope:	yes. i think we need a toast. to a trio of roasted ladies and a narrow opening.

osith: forget-us-knots

the same visions, the same miracles, the same martyrdoms repeated

how to speak in attired words. the viability of expulsion continues into the lucky finds after works. you arrive ailing for no fixed sigh. carrying your severed head under your arm. slip into a fur aperture selling your mind resentfully in a pleasure park. another why some scatter their brains with resolution open a hotel of arches. from arm to a lover. from no harm to a hit. past your rage.

portions of incense, pepper and cinnamon   a silver stylus

it begins in the sea and in grass. in a small quantity of instead of the loaded question. or the loaded stone. a bee falls through a half shut half open. clothed in small loopholes we can in some cynical sense. more than someone strokes me. a wire blazes thus a memory of desire fretting on a cosec. our blinding calculations never reach. alone. white.

we know little that is fact rather than legend

a short introduction to before always. some modesty. instantly forgets the temptation. then triggers the opportunity for a story has behind time. smile. you acquire a sea. what a catastrophe. a force that wavers in the script of your sort of undermining. a skill in dif-ference rather emerges from looking after.

reduced in human memory to an unidentifiable name on a list:

the one whose borders shift; the one who dresses in foam; the junior whose flat drops eaves; the one who sports working days; neither nor not at all the reason; the telephone doctor; the one whose speeches perish with listening; the progressive; the solitary; the corpse in tattered investments; the quickest one to split the second; the dark butter; the shrill may never.

reveal intense loneliness and a sense of isolation

from cliff to cliff three miles away signifiers settle backwards. from the exit or the entrance the view is wrapped in drag. but from the opposite ridge a slight breeze of surprise catches hold of me sucks me up in syllables. my excitement moves sulkily onto the bed. undoing a button at the limit of searching. donate my honour to hide and a cautious speech.

hedwig: my heart in a cracked slipper

angels measure us for a wardrobe of interruptions. and a connoisseur of the senses contemplates the patterns. can you follow with her the echoprints out of the last blue havens? honestly and somehow repropose the particulars for an unorthodox dance in grammatical sandals. all the differently diffident and dependent as the limits of performance. guess its legitimacy as the sperm compete and then clog the speech.

B 4 a *On the left side of the picture, the infirm of all sorts: a man without feet crawls forward with the aid of a hand support, another moves with a crutch and leg support, behind them stand many more supplicants.*

language slings back wanting the maybe. loafing delights. and absence spins slap into the buckled cavity slides through a blizzard of risks. o for the jeopardy of errors embraced in an essay on the pedicuresque.

C 1 b *She climbs to the nun's dormitory and kisses with pious and humble purposefulness every stair and step which the sisters use, likewise the footstools by their beds, yes even the switches with which they flagellate themselves.*

ferocious abstention and toil. suffering heeled in the syntax of stolen and descriptions worn down by refusal. it needs an abstract solitude to wax the damage at the base mention of binding. who will agree to seductions in the name of lend me buttons. all of us trounced out together.

C 3 a *She even sprinkles, especially into her eyes and more often over her whole face, the water in which the sisters have washed their feet.*

the mad of warning. the starved sterilized sexuality of precocious choices. innocents camped on a platform under the derelict influence of a hand writing wedged in between the remedy for too much certainty. the manner in which perhaps the sole authority.

C 3 b *On Maundy Thursday, Hedwig washes, with uncommon love, the feet of lepers, and clothes the lepers, whom she has washed, in new garments.*

form sentences into paragraphs of raffia. peeping wonders in the wardrobe of secrets. pleated replies in a chest of purple suede. someone meowed something limped to the left while in the distance a diluted persuasion persisted until process had pumped time into a flat unconditional. struggle must train in a shrine to the practical disdaining the generic yielding to a gently crafted model of she. (or an analytical enquiry into feminist brogues.) someone's sublime blush improvised the persistence returns. wrapped in a system of nerves quite dada. from plimsoll lines on the temple to ankle ornaments provide a fretwork of harmony.

D 3 a *Barefoot, Hedwig hardens herself in prayer before an altar. Her maid cannot endure the cold. Hedwig invites her to the spot where she has just stood with naked feet. The maid enters, and a pleasant warmth penetrates her.*

now the true story. in bold and cold disguise bliss removed scruples and ideologies. boots of always impeded the body from not even. it left home. through the door of cruelty into a different want. less in disgrace than with a predilection for corrosion. moved out with a shoebox packed with alliterations. transience pulled the cork out of completed. day wore yellow points and the unquiet symptoms of until. beauty watched its curves decompose into the gap roughly between reality and perception. a bell called the hagiographer to the moral design of at once.

D 4 a *Doing penance Hedwig goes yet another day without shoes. Unexpectedly and suddenly her husband appears. The shoes she had she can no longer put on. But she escapes, through a wonder miraculously shod, the anger and reprimands of her husband.*

simplify the bespoken. distil the illusion into a change of subject. the tongue levitates from the weight of can. susurrates with warnings. the wear and tear of a pen charged with the leaks from a bowed body: a donor's body transfusing hot delinquencies of style.

D 5 a *Hedwig kneels before the open door of a church. In biting frost she had come with her ladies-in-waiting to the house of God. The looks and gestures of her companions indicate the bloody prints that Hedwig's naked feet have left in the snow.*

the vectorial case. we could blame our parents. patent thoughts that cool in separation. but a young person opens a boutique full of thresholds. and a professor nonchalantly sabotages the origin with functions in moss green. just a patterned garden of maudlin frisson. a last revenge faded in spectacular starvation. the subject sneaks away in fear of vitality. freshly surrendering to death clad in the courts of a clue.

M 1 b *With the assistance of the saints, Hedwig is received into their company forever. Angels carry her soul to heaven. The nun Martha kneels at the foot of the bed, cured of a chronic desiccation of her mouth and tongue.*

a dilettante for the occasion.

ursula: from the legend of johanna the rigger

and pinnosa had three aunts and three uncles. one uncle was called caspar another handsel but the name of the third has flowed away with the rhine. one of the aunts was called alberta and she was famous across all the oceans for her dancing and for her dress of grey-green elm leaves. another kept her name shrouded in a black cape and was known only by her initials — h.f. — and the third was called wulfhilda and she could multiply drinks. pinnosa had one half-uncle called albrecht whose sister bathild had cut the heads of ten bald invaders. and she had a niece ursula who captained one of the fleet flying a standard embroidered with 81 ermine tails. ursula's sister lewinna accompanied her and she could steer any vessel safely through waves as high as cliffs. wulfhilda had a cousin anadyomene who brought three nieces with her. the first was called aspergilla the second sapientia and the third basilea. and sapientia was also a captain of one of pinnosa's ships and she flew an ensign painted with broken stars. alberta had a niece named in her honour albertina and she had a half-sister johanna renowned throughout the islands for her statues of aphrodite. and johanna had a sister tibba whose voice had raised the living from the dead and whose two nieces also joined the entourage. they were called hannah and ambrosia and were accompanied by their closest friend hendrika who sailed a ship as if she were galloping a horse across a meadow of water. hendrika's aunt joined the crew with her two adopted daughters josepha and huberta.

gorgonia a distant cousin to caspar had a sister carla who had decorated the interior of many shrines to the pregnant river gods. carla had three nieces in the company. one was called eleutheria. another runina. and the third minerva. eleutheria was the fourth leader of the pack and her flag bore a bundle of white branches bursting into flames. eleutheria's uncle gaspard had a half-sister tiberia. she joined her niece and wore a silver mask with a double beard of finely beaten bronze. tiberia had a sister gennaria who could also raise the living from the dead and with her came two brothers casimir and anton and their nieces. these were the twins angelika and henrietta celebrated artists who painted the mastheads in grey red and brown. another brother rieter had a nurse called martha and she also joined the crew bringing the skills she had learnt smuggling bears and goats across rivers in the new world. martha was half-sister to josepha an intimate friend to pinnosa's aunt alberta and she joined the fleet with her niece johanna. and caspar clan-twin to one of pinnosa's uncles had a niece celyndris and she commanded another ship in the squadron whose flag carried a blossoming branch of blue swords. her navigator was called fortunata. cordula born in fingal's cave was the niece of a clockmaker named carl. his sister eugenia was the adopted niece of victoria queen of the land of stone bridges. after victoria's death she was adopted by another queen francesca who ruled a fertile country of wise farms but now she too left its mild shores forever. adolph was brother to wulfhilda's bosom-friend cecilia and had two half-brothers arnold and frank. arnold had a niece gustavia famous for her street-fighting and the pilgrimage she had made to the city of joy. and he had another niece marea whose vineyards were celebrated for their mourning wines. frank also had two nieces paula and wilhelmina the one always seen in her black carpenter's cap the other smoking a pipe. and these four signed up with florentina the fifth of pinnosa's captains. and her flag depicted a crane flying through a dark-grey sky with a train of five-footed crows. florentina had two sisters in her company eugenia and anna. the first was well tutored in all the arts of merlin. anna was as tall as a poplar tree and her silver eyes could see over the horizon. one of florentina's lieutenants was called flora and she was accompanied by her sister maxima. their half-uncle theophilus was a nomad and his sister lucia was another of the ship's captains. her skin was a rich brown leather deeply wrinkled from years of exposure to sun and salt. her flag was stitched together from scraps of bright umbrellas. she was accompanied by the twin sister of her half-brother james. rosalinda was a famous soprano and paula would die in childbirth before our story begins. paula had a brother carl and a sister francesca who built mechanical toys. francesca had a stepmother also called paula who had nine nieces. of these pabula and karla were too young to join the expedition but the other seven followed pinnosa. the first was called georgina and she also loved smoking pipes. the second was called quappi. the third amadoura. and the fourth olga displayed proudly the scars of battles won and lost. the fifth was called arthelia. the sixth juana. and the seventh oscana could bend backwards until the crown of her black head touched her heels. paula also had a cousin mark. he was a temperate man and had a friend samuel whose four nieces joined the navy and always dressed in yellow and black. their names were roberta henrietta alberta and walburga. this last sometimes swapped scarlet for the black. samuel's sister waltruda had her portrait painted by irene whose four nieces josepha erwina edwina and soledad also joined this adventure.

and so the glorious party gathered together and prepared for departure. as i have told you pinnosa had already selected six captains and these were ursula sapientia eleutheria celyndrus florentina and lucia. now she had to select three more to command the remaining vessels. the first was called jotha and her banner bore the image of a thousand-eyed cyclops. she was joined by her two sisters clara and andrea and fourteen of their friends among whom we know the names of only six: achillea waltruda bride georgina sidwell and margaret. the second captain was called carpofora. her ship was shaped like a shark and her silver flag was stitched from the scales of a million fish. josepha brought her friend martina who could turn infinity into form. and martina had two brothers luciano and francesco and these each had one half-niece who joined carpofora's crew. one was called rosemarie and the other was called marlene. and marlene was also known as the magdalene. and she came from egypt and wore gold rings in her ears and nose. and pinnosa's final choice was sibylla niece to her uncle caspar's bosom-friend siegfried. sibylla's flag bore a silver-black spiny sea-snail. sibylla had two sisters with her antonia and susanna. and susanna was joined by two of her closest friends catherine and karen. these are the eleven warriors who led their troops by example and teaching. and now we will tell you of the magicians and priests who travelled with these amazons and later we will also tell you of the many who joined them in other lands.

winifred: lacerated and falling

Enter Teryth from riding, Winifred following.

why do you hover and haunt me? your dead body resisting abbreviations. yonder. beyond nowhere. beyond needs no convincing. o my ancient companion of sparkling distinction. from pulping beliefs issues the will to mix turns endlessly. doors keep. angels tread on treachery. and in my cupboards the spoons cheat. questions glisten with the veneer they have scratched. and would filaments of whenever fill the spaces of unashamed. should we wait to utilize happiness? busy people tumbling into a clever mockery. my mind ladders. decomposes day into diversifications. in the course of within my mind minds. my knees treacle. can you help me move to a considered map?

Scene, a wood, ending in a steep bank over a dry dean.
Winifred having been murdered within, re-enter Caradoc with a bloody sword.

heart where have we been? water falls into the embrace of blades. indeed in deeds immortality. but if we pay attention to the turmoil of the market-women. loathe some reputations. from might to another reason led into a language that whispers. count how many averse facts. how desperate queues outside. or a hostel as home for the minded. gingerly through days of disappointed forms. sit downs something else knows. that these letters may no longer passionately avoid the varieties of ice. foil the demand for honour where a culture of brightness is disposed to electrify the taste of pride. stop and starve. the arm that wrenches me into morning carries me across the freshhold from a bedroom of tissue. and if our despatches miss the fullness of none.

After Winifred's raising from the dead and the breaking out of the fountain.

now while skies blue now while seas salt. and the blue fills with may. we dance with the pilgrims lunge against shuttered views. on crystal breezes proliferate the pointed. matt turns into a jolt of desire. matrimonial crutches. we want them to disappear the kilograms for needy. also to sleep. to deliver us from appropriation. and the wrenches that deprive us of fiascos. not the sight of the sick of the sight. our lungs fill with the miracle questions. and the dancers quit.

henriette delille: requiem for the quadroons of necessity

requiem aeternam dona eis domine
et lux perpetua luceat eis

simplicity in deed reveals a theology meets her silvery laughter ring out into the dance. meets a memory remote and traditional.

kyrie eleison
kyrie eleison

to work with the city's most destitute and deprived people. real actions. a wondrous mixture to guard the house with expectations with holy water and a dusty pink to strengthen entanglements.

quantus tremor est futurus
quando judex est venturus

he took little or no interest in his daughter's speech in a sister's bond in the third's understanding of lists. a woman whose kisses we wrap with the fruit and candy. to apprehend her position in the community to state and note the gossip of endearment. sounds of intelligence sharpened by few choices. unfortunate constitutions of uncertainty everywhere.

liber scriptus proferetum
in quo totum continetur

in which every fact shames its shape: no moonlight tonight but the bent sky glittering with questions. numerous strangers from every country with voices of mandolins and guitars more things than perfect french and courtly grace a genealogy of detonated maxims. we talk in careless absolutes. prefer to taste fervent like angels more numerous than sand. knowledge searching through generic means to womankinds. pillars of rose and gold hints and sways to reach another archives. empowered by pity for the beautiful.

voca me cum benedictus
cor contritum quasi cinis

try a little incognito. said in a lower tone. will you repeat them
with me? la juive leonora elsa aida marguerite sister juliette sister
josephine. and the audience applauded with more warmth than
usual. reprove it all simply. a pale yellow flickering in the great
dark space a song on their lips. practice practice implications in
the womb of time now one's heart. a matter of setting the pearl in
a strange of rumours. in loss of place find frustrated wholeness. for
the sick the infirm and the poor more than speech tears or gestures
could determine.

dies irae dies illa
lacrimosa dies illa

a residue of print to conjecture beyond the song of a mocking bird
in a fragrant orange grove that association for nursing the sick and
destitute with a spacious lack of profit.

dona eis requiem
dona eis requiem

patience when the bayou overflows the capacity to name to go on
to the setting sun of certainty. move move against your own re-
sistance to new scenes new adventures holding on to partially in
stark contrast to an arrogant situation. tossed and tossed spun and
spurned slipped and sleeping in the brown waters of the bayou.

domine jesu christu
rex gloria

bigger than the biggest diamond ring a story to baptize an immense
family of poor aged women. very much wizened and lame. like a
deferred translation. disconnected from the flatness of a noonday

sun with their secrets and friendships stealing in over the heated stillness of principles in a rhythmic chorus of caresses.

hostias et preces
quorum hodie memoriam facimus

perish in the recitation of a quick sympathetic mass. burning and filled with trust without being bound by any vow.

sanctus sanctus sanctus

humanity in all shapes manners forms laughing pushing jostling crowding a mass of women and children judges and doubters.

qui tollis peccata mundi
dona eis requiem

the high quavering of an imperfect tuning fork. or a silent life of opposition. a struggle until the long years of transition and development melt into the heart's tongue.

qui tollis peccata mundi
dona eis requiem

that they may possess the long faint swelling notes of the organ choosing the ruins of enthusiasm. on one of those calm blue-misted balmy november days with a sweet damp wind darned until darn was not the word.

dona eis requiem sempiternam
dona nobis pacem

this thing suddenly this difficulty of identification springing up as fact as weary as rather in the flowered niche above the gold-domed altar. this thing. worn out by work she died. this ugly clumsy analogue of love.

atque ventura ira
dies illa dies irae

i sister now swear those rebellious prayers in a red mouth without an identity in languages of sulky and pouting violets. better than a refuge of afraid. unhabited in the spirited smiles of respect.

in tuo advento suscipiant te martyres
et perducant te

the lost and yellow star points and tears falling like other beads through her rosary onto african roots. after the fragile the dead. with no name but that you give me. no house but my rapidly growing body of spaces.

gertrude and a gertrude and a gertrude is great

or

the colour of the sky is yellow

a butterfly lands on the apocryphal.

gertrude3	paperworks burn in the account.
gertrude1	where we collect the ashes of controversy to charm a path high above the ground flood-deep with visions.
gertrude3	silence taking its shape from the remoteness of compass points.
gertrude1	or the sore laughter of our muffled sisters.
gertrude2	a place where prim seeds conjure their leaves from the acid of bedrocks.
gertrude1	and some sink their roots into jericho's abandoned wells.
gertrude3	until an apparition appeared one deconstructed mourning to parody our promises.
gertrude2	grey walls as borders to the folly of our designs.
gertrude3	i respond traditionally.
gertrude1	sisters who size a relationship. one who dances. one who recoils in more than the corporeal. one who does not agree.

this this one and the latter rise in nervous times in a culture. that this and it swear partings one another. drift into a delayed garden and new spaces in available.

gertrude2   i hear with a slightly cynical smile the languid strokes soften the effect.

gertrude1   the dove of fatigue has landed on a branch of qualms. resupposes.

gertrude3   resonance unfolds in a programme of vain glories.

gertrude1   measure the limit of gold flourishes in the spirit.

gertrude3   i am seriously overdressed.

gertrude2   trust in my dark irises. my fringed purposes for a spring of unclipped effects.

gertrude3   you are philosophers who see the twin in the twin.

gertrude2   one of them is glorious still. one occurs spoiled and uncontrolled. one's works are shabby with inattention and vatic bones.

gertrude3   let me introduce to you my late afternoon companions horrendous and the law.

gertrude2   but i tried to contain ivy's provocations.

the butterfly learns about machinations.

gertrude2   thrift thrives on centuries of eroded histories.

gertrude1   we gather questions. she that gathers least gathers an unread epic. we for the sake of progress quail around a profound inertia.

gertrude3   heroines the significant models for our situation.

laughter again.

gertrude1   our intimacies might realign the brothers in our congregation.

gertrude3   even an orthodox method can leave messy versions.

gertrude2   purchase the anonymous. invent naturalness. for it is goose summer now the spiders are productive.

gertrude1   an unaccompanied nightingale refuses aurora's responsibilities. i thirst unappeased for its lustrous verbs.

gertrude3   our errors are your articles of faith.

gertrude2   excitement cloaked in proprieties.

gertrude3   intercourse of the higher parts. i leave you — the like-minded — this chemistry. a legacy of objects filtered through a sufficient medium. i bequeath you dates as dark as the ashes between reading and pleasing.

at her prime when gertrude one asks he offers her trembling erudition. gertrude two grafts. parsley flourishes wild in the cemetery. not only for modern effects endless experiments. gertrude three delights in the late flowering knotweeds without a precedent.

gertrude3   pining for more than the subtle little sort of differences — influence scraped from the compost store of leftovers.

gertrude2   but we are obliged to trouble getting to know the qualities of cosmopolitans and other elitists.

gertrude3   sometimes a display of arrogance to demonstrate pride.

gertrude2   the height of honesty on the verge of euphorias.

gertrude3   not shadowed by canons and knights.

gertrude2   favourites hidden in trust. purple lances through my chest my heart's tongue throbs. i am wide open to candid lips.

gertrude3   you may generate geographies of perceptions where the unspeakable syncopates.

gertrude1   until everywhere on earth you find independent performances of silence.

gertrude3   like marriage without a husband. or operas without acts.

gertrude1   repetition to compromise the judgements.

the far falls into the marxist deviates.

gertrude1   i shall expose her visions like the concubine misnomer.

gertrude3   by plucking from the manuscripts the unstable uncertainties and collaborations discharged by electrically browed professors.

gertrude1   i fell down at the door of signification and my hands formulated their place on the treacherous.

gertrude3   latin ate a communal manifesto. oversold the reactive sources.

gertrude2   sobriety in the centre surrounded by a flamboyant orthography and a few purpose-filled pages of dragon prose.

gertrude1   i see her in traditional robes quaking like brittle glass. anthologize queerness in a book bound with the burst conundrums of fertility.

gertrude3   anxiously reason emerges through the middle of the afternoon from a paired womb in the matter of a second term.

gertrude2   walking random paths to an exacting spot. my most prized possessions i carry in my hat and edit boldly.

gertrude3   in retrospect it may seem emotional enough.

gertrude1   reporting our lives nothing corresponds to the fall when life's pretexts ripen — the apple and the vine make an intoxicating danger to the very abbess of misery they are inverse and even at the hour of death real.

doubt-filled eli marked her nervous mouth and thought her silent speech not culture but ciphers. and eli asked how long will you parody. put away that nonsense. and hannah replied and said no. i am a modern woman of realistic spirit. yes i have drunk the expressive arabesques and sipped the delicate bromide of theology. with milk. no sugar. but now i hunger for the grace in a name i have weighed before.

gertrude1   i fall with my face to the earth's ear. or this odd passing whim strikes my impressions so that she is carried out.

gertrude2   i obey the sighs in the soil toil for more and less.

gertrude3   i become a prospectus for genial conceit.

gertrude2   a house of water has only evaporating walls for definition. (and flowers for foundations.)

gertrude3   things have never been this overinvested.

gertrude2   i planted hybrids pungent with chance and a dash of cineraria against a sombre hedge of dues.

gertrude3   the eyes are a surprise prodigal with poodles and noodles.

gertrude2   but for a chartered attic built on a gentle autonomy i will go on rambles through the sheltered in wind.

gertrude3   how to become cynosure to act against their material interests.

gertrude2   consider my ephemerals and you will reap the experience of the perennial.

left after all. elementary and ashen.

gertrude3   i grant you the liberty to disagree with her impressions.

gertrude2   contrasting questions and inquiries. channel and medium. deep and obscure.

gertrude1   the dearest relics you can have the words sieved through the holes in my heart.

gertrude3   i want to demonstrate the lasting complications of accuracy.

gertrude2   with oracles or flux or a more sophisticated scheme of hybrid versions edged with actuality.

gertrude1   pursued by history the faceless runner trips over the moment spinning across the path to posterity.

gertrude2   through the smoking archways she explores dawn and dusk: parable and paradise.

gertrude3   an extreme kind of forgets the extremely kind.

gertrude 2   patterns that exercise and exorcise.

gertrude1   love connects disharmonies. who and whom. precious as pregnant. related the i dangles in the amniote. the dead knotted in the matter we bear.

and these letters colourless and cultured in sin. not speech. nor speechless opening like a naked ovary releasing its eggs into a demand for scenes on the other side of read as before.

gertrude1   or come into the contemplation and let me bleed the thing at once. do not these discontinuous accounts of the saints wish.

gertrude2   a vista from groves of dusty lemon to musty orangeries.

gertrude3	a development lined with the vanished. an existence performed of the vanquished.
gertrude1	love the extent in all its borders.
gertrude2	constantly flowing unless the reservoirs become overgrown with neglect.
gertrude3	confident to pursue the cherished into the sea's cast of fast characters.
gertrude1	and i saw a tree growing in the valley of jehosaphat. its roots were cables of confusion. its trunk was stiff with shock. robins nested in its branches of stolen blossom.
gertrude2	perhaps it was an old lime with time-distorted leaves not pollarded but pleached with a hidden sparseness.
gertrude3	if the worsted tree is the community is the statue at liberty.
gertrude2	the pining wood provides the probability needles.

lovers in like and contrasting situations.

gertrude1	i was absorbed by a sign and woke earlier and earlier each morning into the fragrance of violets and dandelions.
gertrude4	the colour of a subject haunts the shadows of before — intensifies them yes but only to those aware of it.
gertrude3	one wonders all the forms a situation doubts.

gertrude2 no lack of bright posies and some ginger humming.

gertrude1 a daily diet of fragments in coriander to keep the confessors at bay.

gertrude3 pure and checkered. some foreigners fill a continent as soonest gone.

gertrude4 united nations of apart from. their appearance matted in the compromise of a role and a past.

gertrude1 o most estimated daughters mortised in our groins.

gertrude2 find repose in this place of peculiar beauty. nots for the eye. ions and antes for the mind.

gertrude1 rapport is prior to rapture novice to decay.

i will quarrel with these inspirations as long as i have learning i will singe my words with the embers of non-words i have my realism.

tight rationing of each delicate letter a neutral logarithm of its reciprocal.

gertrude2 her ears are still firmly on the ground. here. where the tang of evening infiltrates the torn belt around eloquent reallotments lizards play hide and disturb.

gertrude3 where abouts scramble in a bed of undressed humour.

gertrude4 svelte lupins and a cheeky pulse to support my amours propres.

gertrude3   egregious. moderation without limits.

gertrude1   for the verb was married to the blade and nothing could detract the spirit.

gertrude2   the distant view over persephone's fields hidden until one had zigzagged up the hill of language passed through the house of certainties and discovered the occult terraces.

gertrude3   i emigrated i observed i remonstrated. i prescribed the strong drug of period.

gertrude1   but when you accomplish a purpose beyond strength accept it as a deed perceived only in secrets.

gertrude2   a countryside partnership of pruned severity.

gertrude4   leaving in the most provocative overalls from your closet.

              and then came the pope who sickened from eating burnt macaroons.

gertrude1   let my cloistered urbanity guide you.

gertrude2   through an entrance of purblind stone. illusory indeed but also a functional transition privately assembled for the showing.

gertrude1   i am joseph taking the inspeakable and its matter into a sisterland striving to practise the messages.

gertrude2   and to balance the frailty of late-flowering possibilities the margins should be filled to bursting with the textures of reality.

gertrude5   i confirm that i am the nettled process and the hidden subject established in the marrow of that version in exemplarity.

gertrude1   for the poor and for the crazy incognito leaping on the soundtrack of a superficial film.

gertrude5   unabashed caught at the scene of foreswearing the verdicts of comparison for a temporary release.

gertrude1   for does not someone who wishes otherwise to honour a friend extend to her her own garments.

gertrude2   no reward but the shadow of fritillaries.

gertrude5   and my father writes he will agree to reset his jewel against his reverent breast on condition that i renounce all intercourse elsewhere and my correspondence even with my nature.

still the latent will harrow the weak
will reap a speech of wry
novelty fetching a mean price
in the academic markets

when a butterfly beats its wings in the middle ages

gertrude5   i listened so that all seeing it would stare. i assure you touching from inside to inside your crushed objects.

gertrude1   the flowers surrounding me wilt. but someone has sent me seed of the saltwort.

gertrude5   and me the cactus. we are united less by the solidity of our sense than by sampling the grains that swell in it.

gertrude1   and as the one to whom he first appeared i have the dimensions of my misuse and limitations.

gertrude5   he loved the characters of gertrude: her heady conversation her willed presence her slightest opulence.

gertrude1   all beliefs were once as puny as children crossed by a nameless pain. i open wide the wound in his side to replace the nails with cloves.

gertrude5   and i jumped in here to visit your bliss. to watch you raise the monsters. rub your cool fingertips over you couldn't care less.

gertrude1   what a friend. as one who personally leads you through an occlusion filling with autumn leaves and a musk of civilization.

gertrude5   my companion and me whose alarming renaissance was a necessity more chimeric than benevolent.

gertrude1   and when i woke from prayer and responded to my senses i found them rehearsing for tomorrow.

and it came to pass in those ill-disciplined days that she of two names pricked her finger while spinning and fell into a sickness and died. and when those of the new cult had washed her body in citrus juice and fragrant oils they displayed it in an upper chamber. and when the apostle arrived her quilters stood by weeping and showing the robes and shrouds she had sewn. and the envoy decided not to resuscitate a vaunted implausibility.

gertrude1   may the place where the race is run be lapped by
your grace in which i find the most cautious
prizes.

may the cuckoo's tired wings stain my alcove
soft grey the better to appreciate consolation's
colours.

may it be proven empties it.

may my faith in you be a puzzle to you. my dusts
on your recordings.

may it not limit your longings for the limit.

may visions translated into modest stories revise
rituals of romance both ideal and cited.

may that which you investigate last.

may the smoke of the incensed ascend in eigen-
vectors after operations using a style from the
smallest bone of the saint's finger.

may love and november pain.

may. and the virgin rose.

walata petros: rites of resistance in africa

one of the few women saints in ethiopian hagiography, she played a leading role in the anti-catholic struggle waged by the ethiopian mono-physites

for you would not abandon a long tradition of striking women — the queens of the south — nor the red and crescent moon. and your humility drew itself a zone of diverse identities. when one man's grief is another's thorns one woman's skull sifts the authentic for the flavour of meticulously. you saw the miracles of mary ricochet off stone walls and darned the sutures of syncretic into a cranium of cloud.

born in 1594, the daughter of nobility, she longed from childhood for the religious life

we saw you return at sunset and enter the shrine with the jaw of a unicorn. as fatigued as a pregnant elephant. for you had crossed a constellation of tragedy in a cart pulled by hornbills and honey-birds. through your pilgrimage with nightingales as confidantes you drank the sow's resistant milk from a maidenhead horn.

but she became the wife of malkea krestos, one of the leading personalities during the reign of susneyos. she was indifferent to her husband's love and wealth

for the angels rebelled at your birth their tears solidifying to pearls that coil around your neck (and that of a sister princess) like the consolations of philosophy. refugee blood stained your silks and velvets. you know the value of salt. and that to pray is to cross the border of sometimes.

when jesuit missionaries and the ethiopian orthodox clergy initiated their quarrel, walata petros supported the orthodox cause. her husband prevented her first attempt to retire to a convent who wears a filigree of uncertainty? as a child you leapt danced and clapped to the seductive drums of endurance. on this november day possessed of a stranger laughter that disfigures all notions of verity with the patience of a heresy the earth wears a cloak deep blue with courtesy. but the ink condemns the extemporized.

after the rebellion of yolyos in may 1617, the religious conflict entered a new and bitter phase. aged 24, walata petros resolved to end her marriage

but not to relinquish your secret name which claims your content. and cleaves your spirit like a wound inflicting an interim. you could not escape the grace of a squared smile. or a landscape scattered with the black feathers of hope. and the poisonous breeze of disloyalty to whom.

having gathered around her a small group of like-minded women, walata petros moved to waldebba, famous for its hermits and anchorites. however susneyos summoned her and her supporters to court to answer charges brought against them for anti-catholic activities

and your breast is as inviolate as the ark of the covenant set with precious stones. it carries a heart beating with ancient power. there we will find the spelling of simplicity. the dusty abacus that survived the sword. and a grain of mica scorched by persistence.

persecution and confinement followed, the saint and her disciples resisting all efforts to convert them to catholicism

from a mother's rib fused to a preposition. deviations protected by the curves of time. and ecstatic consciousness. no plan but to bequeath indigenous conceptions. dead bodies crowned by brambles near a broken hand.

walata petros was exiled to jabal on the western border of ethiopia. inspired by her courage her guard allowed groups of people to listen to her teachings not as frail as the bones of articulation. churches hewn in rock. protected by remoteness. invested with likelihood. managed by a degree of patience few of us can boast of.

at jabal she established the first of seven communities. the anti-catholic movement gained strength at court

though we have no means to accurately represent a year or a simple prayer. or the intelligence intrinsic to an irregular flower. an outer haven of song. a baptism in miracles. threads of love hanging from the sanctuary's trees.

in 1632 susneyos finally abandoned the bitter struggle to impose the roman catholic faith in ethiopia. walata petros was allowed to return to lake tana

lend us your high pitch. that we can puncture the grey prospect of indifference. draw into our needles rhythms as blue as your nile and as agitated. we stand at the border of a false capacity. bake promises in the house of bread.

the new emperor fasilidas restored the ethiopian monophysite faith. during the last 12 years of her life, walata petros travelled the country teaching, gathering new disciples and founding new religious communities

are these scenes compulsed by illegitimacy? what sullen arrogance compels us to place them in the seventeenth rather than the twentieth (or the minus tenth) century? we rode here on the camel's trait to affiliate with disappearance. and dance around your tomb as in the days of solomon and sheba to the sound of lutes and sistras. bathed by the ashen moonlight falling from an icon of continuities.

walata petros died on 24 november 1643 and was buried on the holy island of rema near the south-east shore of lake tana

catherine: rites of part(ur)ition

for c.m.

the best description could hardly produce a faithful portrait even if it closely resembled the original
preemptress of your own enlightenment. what you need to inflict the vulgar on a world of stuck-up faces. scared and snared by your own regard and yet silly once happy subject really meant coping with tin gods (what colour were your hair?). now through the door-frames averse scripts imperfect the distempered walls. foolish and fond laugh in the shadows a wild peace waits in the wings of in-security every entrance equally eloquent and empty. as we try to design a convention on the delta of words construct a stage flooded with caustic celebrations.

in due time you will come to my palace
as a pretense yes as relaxed as outside the limits of the experts' confidence. dive into my cosmetic bag of vulnerable eye-liner and smudgesticks. borrow my hats protect the silence of a trappist's reputation. let's redress the effeminate suffering substantially. here's a tissue to confront your features : bless your s-catology. and your scripture of defecated nouns. the dissident invective to clean out your choc-a-bloc tones. when the king offered her land and pos-sessions the saint chose reflections and pieces of infinitely fragile bone. and as i watch you pinching that zone of lavish attempts oh the desire to lean into endurance (the sadists will always come with their sharp points) on parole marked by stumbling. wirrwar — yes we are.

she will act more prudently if she lets herself be convinced by you. recognizes her
error. where dead princesses love the statement itches. enclosed in habit sari or sarong you could absorb your identity in potential rules. there were more than genes in your ovum. tangling with the dead and fabulous entranced by the spare notes everywhere

— surprise survived — perceived only in terms of an inability to smile and inhale your own simile. when calypso or ceres (or maybe even andromeda) got drunk on the best ale sappho could brew for her do you think she sang to pay her taxes (to reinforce the walls around the crumbling city) or chanted her dischords at a mounted policeman who thought he'd arrested an escaped tasmanian devil? the crowd hurries by bent by aren't we. aber wir tragen unsere arbeit doppelseitig.

time passed.
et na und? i want to know the complexion of a glance how an arm let you search for ghosts how the sparrows learnt to read. when a fig fell into a glass of cider when you perceived a lonely butterfly dance through the signs of a bonfire (we don't need a camera) when love was a culinary art bold enough to fry oranges (perhaps memory loss is like rickets a softening of the brain caused by a deficiency in vitamin D is for dangerous). where your affected nerves untuned by negligence went at what a(c)cost where politeness flies and where nayture can put us on the write path. (or could i suggest you try going to bed with a vampire?)

these fragments fall on those present. brains are split open.
they call it "nonnenarbeit" the attempt to take the hazelnut out of the rosary daub it with spittle hang it round the neck of the venus de milo (the question sounds like a laughing eyebrow) deliberately depart from the censors in the art market (wearing venial masks) to the edge of praise. mary has torn her lazy blue gown two many times what the heck i want to get married in a bright red veil to the girl who graduated à la mode of her class in the school for frivolous verses (and at the reception we'll serve you fake caviar — tapioca dipped in dominican ink — and cassandra's iced screams). what you do not possess you cannot return. divine and trivial go hand in hand to the altered.

the sides are not equal
on a shroud sewn with threads of emeralds preserve the past. perhaps aida chose wisely — it's quieter in a tomb. fine confusion in

the spider's mockery. licking the milk from stone walls. o sweet
genetics. but i need to plunge deeper. to the sima — that crust
of silence and magnanimity (the bed of friendship). then deeper
still to a burning discontinuity. from down here i can send you a
postcard of crushed caraway seeds. and since you suggest we need
new scenarios and librettos perhaps i'd better set this operettis-
sima in the peru of my imagination disappear into its gyroscape
of marean clamour and prolix outcrops of late in understanding.
but i'll freeze in blue smiles. oh for the solemn insanity of quarrels.
the witch leaves an apologetic sentry in the foothills of grammar. a
parrot's green feather falls from her lips. suddenly i feel like eating
the negative promises of henbane. scratch the mother as cicatrix on
the nun's laudanum air. quicker than

silver when mixed with lead cannot be changed

barbara: sinking done into funeral waters

come to shroud me where the rain meets the eye under an anaemic sky. a filament of youth moves into apostasy and a ballerina's leg outskirts a council of the perished. we chiselled still illuminations while building with a germ of certain to reach a massive yield of dead body. a maiden with the manners of marble — incredibly blond — meditated on the discovered. the sea functions mature into strikes. readily take the direction of branding.

question much the costume of brutality and unbelievers founding spare accounts. liberations forsake calms. an "adolescent" adds a porch to adore. the smallest condition for joined. daughters date this day daringly. scheme at it. include luscious rubrics lubriciously ambivalent and ludicrously sapphic. almost poetry. OUR COUNTRY UNSURE OF OUR COUNTRY! de-serving servants see me mediate means. a scene of the silver-sick tarnished in silent. stand in tending towards everything including the rug. disrobed whipped into a cream of descending did. such suitors fell off surprised.

subtle wreaths of hair plaited with laughter to the frayed ends of not even. the reason appropriates the appropriate. all her heart all windows into the all. disordered deeds ride into piecefully. a stranger strawberry shade of honour. querulous however at the final analysis. a mind of minds and mistakes mothers a friend afterwards — courage. later than lambs and the law. from perfectly formed high personages to three persons ignorant of a fate fatale to relate. bold enough. every time and time again of many times.

the mystery the sign a condition of desiring generates the reason why. lovers in the dark forget forms to eradicate. rabble at degree eleven. close combat repairs into the calm of daylight. the closedness of savour. paradise enter paradise incredibly distorted by the muted sharpened by pain contrive to possess how much. doors reshut. depend on meditating discovered not to obey readily.

my outward soul lashes the fair lady to the last. a version of desires viscous with weariness. but neither strength neither harm neither rest. moves will meanwhile into philosophy readily. engraves the performance of tender surliness with holy disenchantment. however at home. if we wear out well we can keep bursting with laughter. if we wear in as many an old retired aunt with weak hearts. sweet hard sweethearts and mistresses of the mistake at midnight.

heaven being gone we found a country found cross channels read under burning lamps that might land in later. the punished put to the pursuit of performing irritably. we daughtered the daily each day hugging our thoughts of vaulting over contemporary. kittens or functions. must we decide we must. persons imperfect. extrakin. questions multiplied in requesting the middle aged in quires. whose ordeals once ordered smart under value emanating from even every person perfect lies because person ages by pedigrees change christ. chased among angels of stone.

leave this to control what will will not. but the direction of branding the standing motivated by other forms set out on feet. under the slivered sign of sides. testing learned to leave by leaving. every dream eagerly endowed with a perfume takes unawares. under heavily masked lashes a lady came last night loyal to units of further. but a delay desperate to describe. a word lasts so long as it deputizes for curious. beauty depends on where you look. just at the foot of an ice pyre time came. niece to proper time and every time arriving reluctantly.

from dissolutions we wear somebodies between the poles of point and polite. my nose twitches suspiciously in the noble gas of now inspired with love. the loved love looking. always awkwardly dressed. who never fits vagabond incompleteness. they also all sorts of alone. neither chases neither changes neither descend (did they did not) into a secret shivering watching snow fall with a passion for structures.

we might disorder the ride into paradigms. we could wear our discourse of particulars in parodies of incredibly proper. the neat and the new running eastward expensively eastward. around an excommunicating peace promising calm and a frightening tranquillity.

leocadia and raquel: toledo

time: 9 a.m. on the 9th day of december in the present.

place: the synagogue converted into the church of santa maria la blanca now in ruins. a large chess board pierces the borders. leocadia (died circa 304) dancing and working. whose fair hair recollects the design of holiness. stillness proceeds from the moors' arches. a few devils march past the window of ordinates. leocadia applies energy to a soft embroidery.

enter raquel (disappeared 1492) from the side.

leocadia: (introspectively) welcome raquel.

raquel: blessed art thou who brightens the parts we play in these spaces.

leocadia: a droll effect.

raquel: i have come to acquire perceptions. acquire rhymes. acquire the shriek of consequences.

leocadia: you know how apostles die?

raquel: by filling the place of imperatives. flying into a reason of ice.

leocadia walks to the shattered altar and makes the sign of fragility with a finger on a stone in the wall.

raquel: (in a tone stamped with intimacy) i choose violation.

leocadia: this mark will remain impressed until the extremities.

raquel: as if leaving amongst ease and heritage.

leocadia: as if traced on wax or soft clay.

raquel: in a laboratory of fantasies and activities.

leocadia: (with a voice petrified in the shadows) tell me raquel you have lovers?

raquel: some. i value their colours in absence. their transgressions with ambiguity. their burning effigies.

leocadia: i beg your pardon for my designs.

raquel takes the whole material and studies it.

raquel: the blessed sacrament in white.

leocadia: i think they threw me from a high rock.

raquel: woman lived in fear of her life. if she had initially rehearsed the situation knowingly. but they accepted and limited.

the nave fills with beaten light. supporting one another raquel and leocadia fasten the needlework into the aisles. with letters from the world they mount the larchwood.

*

on the church porch
        something held my will
                wears the restraints of stranged

during the christian reconquest, the rights of individuals and communities were subject to constant change, mosques and synagogues were either destroyed or turned into churches, but the old synagogue inside the walls of toledo was repaired

with tools to change
     what ghosts open

at the height of its prosperity the size of the community has been estimated at around 12,000 — one third of the total population — with ten synagogues

so that a particular quenches
     an obscurity

1,200 jewish children, women and men of the alcana quarter died in the persecutions of 1355... 8,000 toledo jews died during the siege of henry of trastamara in 1368

descending the overcrowdedslope
     to voice

jews were imprisoned in their synagogues until they paid a special tax

the sorrow of walking through rage
     and still mysterious managing to raise
          a small town around faded
stones. a town of blind lanes
     leading into lanes
          inlayed with silver

she said she had lied in her confession because she was afraid of being tortured. she then began to refuse food in prison, and her imprisoned husband's efforts to console her by shouting to her from his cell were of no avail. due to her growing derangement she was removed from the prison in secret. two days later she committed suicide by throwing herself into a well

when home becomes a line
    of oneself
        in their

an underground passage along the outer edge of the juderia is said to have been used by both jews and conversos to escape persecution

marked and about
    flow together. a graceful drought
        deletes the last changes
what ages an artist
    into an evangelist

"The fire has been kindled, and it will burn until not one of them is left alive."

*

time: sunset on the 9th day of december in the present.

place: my kitchen in basel. raquel wears something promising. leocadia's relics move without fear of sound. raquel watches leocadia.

raquel: (laughing) i had a child of pauses. (unwinding a scroll of gloss) and spent the morning curdling milk.

leocadia: i long for the monastery.

raquel: i inhabit the checks of mockery.

leocadia: (pouring out champagne) a study in white restoration.

raquel: or in stone enunciations.

leocadia: you have whereas. you eat moments and what you eat merges with what you approach. the strongest evening.

we drink the champagne.

leocadia: you shall not repent your achievements and must cry out all day and all night without rest to the world.

raquel: in the pursuit of wishes growing into the emptiness. we have a lonely brittleness.

leocadia: (watching me icing cinnamon stars with saffron) you will really eat all those? your effect overtakes disappointment. i have a hunger.

raquel: you too? what fines for indignity and blemish and pain?

me: speech pruned and melted to succeed.

leocadia: (to raquel and me) and what will you desire?

raquel: your mantilla to wrap their ambitions into many moulds.

me: (writing) a life.

frances xavier cabrini: the villa without a toilet

how not to disdain the later questions when we come through the port of atavism watched by a guarded aversion. scarred cheeks turn an olive smile into ivoried sorrow. erect in our exclusions we stand in serrated queues of silence our education leased to the vital conservation of somatic intentions. hope is like a spermatozoon losing its head in that decisive moment when the spirit encounters a strange emancipation. the violence of abbreviations. listen to the civil officials in uniform brushing off that dusty strangeness into piles of untidy totalities. as if a person is a venetian blind on the façade of an empty house penetrated through the cracks of self-contact by the city's ataxia. the protester in surprise lives in the flesh of an infant probability. suave and sticky as recriminations the saints and the grand old men of torah dance in the unpacked drone of the immigrant never and forever extended into every dead body. the poets of nostalgia and radical beginnings spit untoward across the acid margins of hostility. their noisy variety of doubts feed the attorneys specific and saturated facts like the host the guest double-bonded in risky languages. centimetering the rails. the poets' slow vigil defining stranger at the checkpoint of inherited attitudes. a candle stutters in the soft wind of vertigo. occipital eyes aside. inhale the noon the frost and the angels.

*   *   *   *   *

stretched between the family and the vast recipe book of desires she breaks eggs into the flour of sensations. in abandoned houses plants an arch of perennials over the ditch of means. this is what we want exclusively to hear the wing of the eagle fluttering in fatigue. tenacious and considering through english oozing out of sheltered places like sugar in apple pie. these are the damaged hours. all the same all in a different style of black shawls. sometimes squalid sometimes surprisingly moral confusing our lovers you and me. taking an immense step back into obscurity. into the science of the grave where the spices sit next to the stained volumes of poetry.

foods whose preparation requires conformation to the tin require-
ments of estrangement. when the plaster saints begin to simmer.
when naked women start to swim in birdbaths of ginger. when the
sower of seems kisses the open ropeveined hands neither our lips
nor our smiles can escape the gathering of ashes.

*   *   *   *

we return to a greener verdict.

           the cypresses have run down to the gulf
of horizons.

                               imagine
the small phenomenon of paper fins.

the scroll of mary

memories meet memories abandoned and shed as brown
pigments flake meticulously from walls . i recognize your upraised
eyes and downturned mouth as if the throne you affirm resents
the weight of weary bones and a uterus hence silent . you
travelled many many miles across a landscape of veiled valleys .
rough tracks . your ass retching on dust . in darkness . though you
had conceived in may sunshine made a yellow ball of holy vomit
each dawn tossed the pain through a closed door . girls learned early
to simulate dreams married to endurance . you never told anyone
what the angel had promised : twins : girl and boy : god's copy .
late one morning on that cataclysmic path to bethlehem
despite joseph's quiet disfigured hand on its frayed reins the tired
donkey tripped and tumbled . mary — you braced — then also
fell — heavily . one heart stopped beating . forever . tonight nearly
2000 years ago you aborted . birthed . mourned

cinnabar and indigo . plant with mineral . robes stained by the
earth drawing deep blue tracks through the gently black was
missing . maybe tablets released from yesterday needs your
sanguine cloak draws a gaze down blind corridors maddened by
the spirit of whereas your smile still equals a damage . not the
eyes but landscapes of an earth scorched so so dry that water
mirrors miracles . and how roses save priests . ruby or garnet settings
ancient in their power as mercurial as infrequent as abbesses . and
i wonder if the monk woken abruptly from his dreams hungry saw
a matrix crumble . what memory against collapse mixes matches
and fixes rules as walls yearning for a tomb among corpses near to
none muffled by an irregular uniform skilled hands daily copy and
combine intelligence with restraint . disappearance absorbs into its
greys the last menstruation

my ! what handsome guardian angels . experts style this form
gunda gunde : a few fine miniature variations on an idiosyncratic
model . demanding from a late-20th-century european seeing
"elongated eyes" flat heads spatula-shaped faces to resist

suggesting the artist metabolized imported "eastern even far eastern influences." you'd think a painter an exacting gifted irascible ethiopian maker of divine images possessed no means of inspiration other than mimicry . your foreheads recede mary until we arrive at illuminating failures . and those tiger-toothed lightning beams screaming across your dress would look pretty on chinese dragons . as for the missing halo i'm more inclined to accept the obvious admittedly unverified idea of symbolic resistance . for emperor zara yaequob your devoted and zealous advocate brutally persecuted that heretic stefanite community simply because they refused to prostate themselves before your image though they painted it with an elegance mesmeric in the strange attributes confusion

a family fleeing wrapped in darkling air thick with african ciphers . he whimpers to the steady slap of soles on stone sand and silent track . their source and their destination : distance . departing . the smell of roast meat worms the memory clings to almond soup . proud human voices burn . eyes squint through a dust-drawn genealogy . the dust that dances madly with the patience of perhaps we will wake from under this dreaming text walks in the directions its margins display and contain yellow borders on her metaphorion . as the appearance perishes you notice her eyes have arrived and the old sky has torn right through with thorns of shadow . or that separating salt from water would rescue the present in mistaking the future for a remote word . time drunk slowly like salome's riddle a gourd of orpiment cast from black ground licked by mothers searching for graves . solitude billows from each gesture betrays friendship between a staggering cloud of ash and a million oleander blossoms . we accept ancestors . narrate the meeting of stranger and name as if sharpening a hidden instrument on horizons of a misty standard . neither islands in the oceans nor lakes in the craters of mountains . when some have left the mass all are left in the leavings

Bibliography

General

Amt, Emilie (ed) (1993) *Women's Lives in Medieval Europe: A Sourcebook.* London, Routledge

Anson, John (1974) The female transvestite in early monasticism: the origin and development of a motif. *Viator* 5:1–32

Atkinson, Clarissa, Constance H. Buchanan and Margaret R. Miles (eds) (1985) *Immaculate and Powerful: the Female Image and Social Reality.* Boston, Beacon

Attwater, Donald (1983) *The Penguin Dictionary of Saints*, 2nd edn. London, Longman

Barratt, Alexandra (ed) (1992) *Women's Writing in Middle English.* London, Longman

Bell, Rudolph M. (1985) *Holy Anorexia.* Chicago, University of Chicago Press

Berman, Constance H., Charles W. Connell and Judith Rice Rothschild (eds) (1985) *The Worlds of Medieval Women: Creativity, Influence, Imagination.* Morgantown, West Virginia University Press

Bornstein, Daniel and Robert Rusconi (eds) (trans. Margery J. Schneider) (1996) *Women and Religion in Medieval and Renaissance Italy.* Chicago, University of Chicago Press

Bibliotheca Sanctorum (1961) Rome, Istituto Giovanni XXIII nella Pontificia Università Lateranense

Brother Kenneth (1976) *Saints of the Twentieth Century.* London, Mowbray

Bynum, Caroline Walker (1987) *Holy Feast and Holy Fast: The Religious Significance of Food to Medieval Women.* Berkeley, University of California Press

Bynum, Caroline Walker (1991) *Fragmentation and Redemption: Essays on Gender and the Human Body in Medieval Religion.* New York, Zone

Bynum, Caroline Walker, Stevan Harrell and Paula Richman (eds) (1986) *Gender and Religion: On the Complexity of Symbols.* Boston, Beacon

Cherewatuk, Karen and Ulrike Wiethaus (1993) *Dear Sister: Medieval Women and the Epistolary Genre.* Philadelphia, University of Pennsylvania Press

Cloke, Gillian (1995) *This Female Man of God: Women and Spiritual Power in the Patristic Age, AD 350–450.* London, Routledge

Crownfield, David R. (1992) *Body/Text in Julia Kristeva: Religion, Women, and Psychoanalysis.* Albany, State University of New York Press

De Sola Chervin, Ronda (1991) *Treasury of Women Saints.* Cork, Mercier

Dronke, Peter (1984) *Women Writers of the Middle Ages: A Critical Study of Texts from Perpetua (+203) to Marguerite Porete (+1310).* Cambridge, Cambridge University Press, 1984

Dunbar, Agnes B.C. (1904) *A Dictionary of Saintly Women.* London, Bell

Elm, Susanna (1994) *Virgins of God: The Making of Asceticism in Late Antiquity.* Oxford, Clarendon, pp 255–281

Erler, Mary and Maryanne Kowaleski (1988) *Women and Power in the Middle Ages.* Athens, University of Georgia Press

Farmer, David Hugh (1992) *The Oxford Dictionary of Saints*, 3rd edn. Oxford, Oxford University Press

Hall, James (1974) *Dictionary of Subjects and Symbols in Art.* London, Murray

Histoire des saints et de la sainteté chrétienne (1986) C.SS.R. Paris, Hachette

Kieckhefer, Richard and George D. Bond (1988) *Sainthood: Its Manifestations in World Religions.* Berkeley, University of California Press

Lamperis, Linda and Sarah Stanburg (eds) (1993) *Feminist Approaches to the Body in Medieval Literature.* Philadelphia, University of Pennsylvania Press

Larrington, Carolyne (1995) *Women and Writing in Medieval Europe.* London, Routledge

MacDonald, Margaret Y. (1996) *Early Christian Women and Pagan Opinion: The Power of the Hysterical Woman.* Cambridge, Cambridge University Press

Matter, E. Ann and John Coakley (eds) *Creative Women in Medieval and Early Modern Italy: A Religious and Artistic Renaissance.* Philadelphia, University of Pennsylvania Press

McNamara, Jo Ann Kay (1996) *Sisters in Arms.* Cambridge, Harvard University Press

Newman Williams, Marty and Anne Echols (1994) *Between Pit and Pedestal: Women in the Middle Ages.* Princeton, Wiener

Pagels, Elaine (1982) *The Gnostic Gospels.* London, Penguin

Perkins, Judith (1995) *The Suffering Self: Pain and Narrative Representation in the Early Christian Era.* London, Routledge

Petroff, Elizabeth Alvida (1986) *Medieval Women's Visionary Literature.* Oxford, Oxford University Press

Petroff, Elizabeth Alvida (1994) *Body and Soul: Essays on Medieval Women and Mysticism.* Oxford, Oxford University Press

Ridyard, Susan J. (1988) *The Royal Saints of Anglo-Saxon England.* Cambridge, Cambridge University Press

Salisbury, Joyce E. (1991) *Church Fathers, Independent Virgins.* London, Verso

Stuard, Susan Mosher (ed) (1987) *Women in Medieval History and Historiography.* Philadelphia, University of Pennsylvania Press

Walker, Barbara G. (1983) *The Women's Encyclopedia of Myths and Secrets.* San Francisco, HarperSan Francisco

Walsch, Michael (ed) (1985) *Butler's Lives of the Saints: New Concise Edition.* Tunbridge Wells, Burns & Oates

Wyschogrod, Edith (1990) *Saints and Postmodernism: Revisioning Moral Philosophy.* Chicago, University of Chicago Press

Young, Serenity (1993) *An Anthology of Sacred Texts by and about Women.* London, Pandora

Angela
Steegman, Mary G. (trans) *The Book of Divine Consolation of the Blessed Angela of Foligno*. New York, Cooper Square

Anne Line
Latz, Dorothy (1989) *"Glow-worm Light": Writings of 17th Century English Recusant Women from Original Manuscripts*. Salzburg, Institut für Anglistik und Amerikanistik

Perpetua
Franz, Marie-Louise von (1980) *The Passion of Perpetua*. Irving, Spring

Mother Maria Skobtsova
Hackel, Sergei (1965) *One, of Great Price: The Life of Mother Maria Skobtsova, Martyr of Ravensbruck*. London, Darton, Longman and Todd
Hackel, Sergei (1981) *Pearl of Great Price: The Life of Mother Maria Skobtsova 1891–1945*. London, Darton, Longman and Todd
Saward, John (1980) *Perfect Fools: Folly for Christ's Sake in Catholic an Orthodox Spirituality*. Oxford, Oxford University Press

Mary the Egyptian
Benedicta Ward SLG (1987) *Harlots of the Desert: A Study of Repentance in Early Monastic Sources*. London, Mowbray

Juliana
Johannes Paul II (1996) *EWIG* nos 3+4:11
Newman, Barbara (trans) (1988) *The Life of Juliana of Mont-Cornillon*. Toronto, Peregrina
Rubin, Miri (1991) *Corpus Christi: The Eucharist in Late Medieval Culture*. Cambridge, Cambridge University Press
Snoek, G.J.C. (1995) *Medieval Piety from Relics to the Eucharist: A Process of Mutual Interaction*. Leiden, Brill

Pandita Ramabai
Johnsen, Linda (1994) *Daughters of the Goddess: The Women Saints of India*. St. Paul, Yes International
Lopez, Donald S. Jr (ed) (1995) *Religions of India in Practice*. Princeton, Princeton University Press

Dietrich Bonhoeffer
Bonhoeffer, Dietrich (1986–1999) *Werke;* hrsg. von Eberhard Bethge. München, Chr. Kaiser.
Bonhoeffer, Dietrich und Maria von Wedemeyer (1992) *Brautbriefe Zelle 92: 1943–1945;* hrsg. von Ruth-Alice von Bismarck. München, Beck

Sor Juana Inés de la Cruz

Arenal, Electa (1983) The convent as catalyst for autonomy: two Hispanic nuns of the seventeenth century. In: Miller, Beth (ed) *Women in Hispanic Literature: Icons and Fallen Idols.* Berkeley, University of California Press, pp 147–183

Franco, Jean (1989) *Plotting Women: Gender and Representation in Mexico.* London, Verso

Merrim, Stephanie (ed) (1991) *Feminist Perspectives on Sor Juana Inés de la Cruz.* Detroit, Wayne State University Press

Sayers Peden, Margaret (trans.) (1987) *A Woman of Genius: The Intellectual Autobiography of Sor Juana Inés de la Cruz,* 2nd edn. Salisbury, Lime Rock

Tavard, George H. (1991) *Juana Inés de la Cruz and the Theology of Beauty: The First Mexican Theology.* Notre Dame, University of Notre Dame Press

Kateri Tekakwitha

Allen, Paula Gunn (1986) *The Sacred Hoop: Recovering the Feminine in American Indian Traditions.* Boston, Beacon

Allen, Paula Gunn (1989) *Spider Woman's Granddaughters.* London, Women's Press

Anderson, Karen (1991) *Chain Her by One Foot: The Subjugation of Women in Seventeenth-Century New France.* London, Routledge

Boyle, David (1985) The pagan Iroquois. In: Tooker, Elizabeth (ed) *An Iroquois Source Book, vol 2. Calendric Rituals.* New York, Garland, pp 54–196

Brown, Judith K. (1970) Economic organization and the position of women among the Iroquois. *Ethnohistory* 17:151–167

Koppedrayer, K.I. (1993) The making of the first Iroquois virgin: early Jesuit biographies of the blessed Kateri Tekakwitha. *Ethnohistory* 40(2): 277–306

Shimony, Annemarie (1985) Iroquois religion and women in historical perspective. In: Yazbeck Haddad, Yvonne and Ellison Banks Findly (eds) *Women, Religion, and Social Change.* Albany, State University Press of New York, pp 397–418

Shoemaker, Nancy (1995) Kateri Tekakwitha's tortuous path to sainthood. In: Shoemaker, Nancy (ed) *Negotiators of Change: Historical Perspectives on Native American Women.* London, Routledge, pp 49–71

Snow, Dean R. (1994) *The Iroquois.* Oxford, Blackwell

Steckley, John (1992) The warrior and the lineage: Jesuit use of Iroquoian images to communicate Christianity. *Ethnohistory* 39(4):478–509

Zemon Davis, Natalie (1994) Iroquois women, European women. In: Hendricks, Margo and Patricia Parker (eds) *Women, "Race," and Writing in the Early Modern Period.* London, Routledge, pp 243–258

Wiborada

Berschin, Walter (ed) *Vitae Sanctae Wiboradae*. St. Gallen, Historische Verein des Kantons St. Gallen

Keller, Stefan (1993) *Grüningers Fall: Geschichten von Flucht und Hilfe*. Zürich, Rotpunkt

Domitilla

Jones, C. Brian W. (1992) *The Emperor Domitian*. London, Routledge

Stevenson, J. (1978) *The Catacombs: Rediscovered Monuments of Early Christianity*. London, Thames and Hudson

Julian

Glasscoe, Marion (1993) *Julian of Norwich: 'Endless Knowying of God'*. In: *English Medieval Mystics: Games of Faith*. Harlow, Longman, pp 215–267

Caterina

Nugent, Donald Christopher (1987) Saint Catherine of Genoa: Mystic of pure love. In: Wilson, K.M. (ed) *Women Writers of the Renaissance and Reformation*. Athens, University of Georgia Press, pp 67–80

Maria Maddelena de'Pazzi

Riccardi, Antonio (1994) The mystic humanism of Maria Maddelena de'Pazzi (1566–1607). In: Matter, E. Ann and John Coakley (eds) *Creative Women in Medieval and Early Modern Italy: A Religious and Artistic Renaissance*. Philadelphia, University of Pennsylvania Press, pp 212–236

Jeanne d'Arc

Barstow, Anne Llewellyn (1986) *Joan of Arc: Heretic, Mystic, Shaman*. Lewiston, Mellen

Duby, Georges et Andrée (1973) *Les procès de Jeanne d'Arc*. Paris, Gallimard/Juillard

Pernoud, Régine (1962) *Jeanne d'Arc par elle-même et par ses témoins*. Paris, Seuil

Röckelein, Hedwig, Charlotte Schoell-Glass and Maria E. Müller (1996) *Jeanne d'Arc oder wie Geschichte eine Figur konstruiert*. Freiburg, Herder

Wheeler, Bonnie and Charles T. Wood (eds) (1996) *Fresh Verdicts on Joan of Arc*. New York, Garland

Modwenna

Baker, A.T. and Alexander Bell (1947) *St. Modwenna*. Oxford, Anglo-Norman Text Society/Blackwell

Price, Jocelyn (1988) *La Vie de Sainte Modwenne*: a neglected Anglo-Norman hagiographic text, and some implications for English secular literature. *Medium Ævum* 47:172–189

Wogan-Browne, Jocelyn (1992) Queens, virgins and mothers: hagiographic representations of the abbess and her powers in twelfth- and thirteenth-century Britain. In: Fradenburg, Louise Olga (ed) *Women and Sovereignty*. Edinburgh, Edinburgh University Press, pp 14–35

Anne Askew

Askew, Anne (1546/1547//1996) The first examination of Anne Askew, with elucydation of J. Bale. The lattre examination of Anne Askew, with the elucydation of J. Bale. In: King, John N. (selected and introduced)/Betty S. Travitsky, Patrick Cullen (general eds) *The Early Modern English woman: A Facsimile Library of Essential Works. Part 1: Printed Writings, 1500–1640. Volume 1. Anne Askew*. Aldershot, Scolar

Margaret of Antioch

Cazelles, Brigitte (1991) *The Lady as Saint: A Collection of French Hagiographic Romances of the Thirteenth Century*. Philadelphia, University of Pennsylvania Press, pp 216–237

Mary Magdalene

Wilson R. McL. and George W. McRae (1979) The Gospel According to Mary. BG, 1:7,1–19,5. In: Parrott, Douglas M. (vol ed) Nag Hammadi Codices V, *2–5* and VI with Papyrus Berolinensis 8502, *1* and *4*. Leiden, Brill, pp 453–471

Faith, Hope and Charity

Saint Augustine (trans. Louis A. Arand) (1947) *Faith, Hope and Charity*. Westminster, New Bookshop

Osith

Fell, Christine, Cecily Clark and Elizabeth Williams (1984) *Women in Anglo-Saxon England and the Impact of 1066*. London, British Museum Publications

Hedwig

Metzger, Konrad und Franz (Übers.) (1967) *Das Leben der heiligen Hedwig*. Düsseldorf, Patmos

Nigg, Walter (1991) *Hedwig von Schlesien*. Würzburg, Echter

Ursula

Zehnder, Frank Günter (1978) *Die H. Ursula und Ihre Elftausend Jungfrauen*. Cologne, Wallraf-Richartz Museum

Zehnder, Frank Günter (1985) *Sankt Ursula: Legende, Verehrung, Bilderwelt*. Cologne, Wienand

Winifred

Bord, J. & C. (1985) *Sacred Waters: Holy Wells and Water Lore in Britain and Ireland*. London, Granada

Hopkins, Gerard Manley (1990) *The Poetical Works of Gerard Manley Hopkins*. Oxford, Clarendon

Henriette Delille

Bryan, Violet Harrington (1993) *The Myth of New Orleans in Literature: Dialogues of Race and Gender*. Knoxville, University of Tennessee Press

Clayton, Ronnie W. (1990) *Mother Wit: The Ex-Slave Narratives of the Louisiana Writers' Project*. New York, Lang

Dunbar-Nelson, Alison (1988) *The Works of Alice Dunbar-Nelson* (repr.) ed. Gloria T. Hull. New York, Oxford University Press

Gould, Virginia Meacham and Charles E. Nolan (1998) *Henriette Delille: Servant of Slaves*. New Orleans, Sisters of the Holy Family

Hall, Gwendolyn Midlo (1992) *Africans in Colonial Louisiana: The Development of Afro-Creole Culture in the Eighteenth Century*. Baton Rouge, Louisiana State University Press, 1992

Gertrude

Finnigan, Mary Jeremy (1991) *The Women of Helfta: Scholars and Mystics*. Athens, University of Georgia Press

Gertrude the Great of Helfta (trans. Gertrude Jaron Lewis and Jack Lewis) (1989) *Spiritual Exercises*. Kalamazoo, Cistercian Publications

Spitzlei, Sabine B. (1991) *Erfahrungsraum Herz: Mystik des Zisterzienserinnenkloster Helfta in 13. Jahrhundert*. Stuttgart-Bad Cannstall, frommann-holzboog

Talmage, Frank (1986) Apples of god: the inner meaning of sacred texts in medieval Judaism. In: Green, Arthur (ed) *Jewish Spirituality: From the Bible through the Middle Ages*. London, Routledge and Kegan Paul, pp 313–355

Walata Petros

(see also Mary)

Frend, W.H.C. (1972) *The Rise of the Monophysite Movement: Chapters in the History of the Church in the Fifth and Sixth Centuries*. Cambridge, Cambridge University Press

Johnson, Samuel (ed. Joel J. Gold) (1985) *A Voyage to Abyssinia* (translated from the French). New Haven, Yale University Press

Sumner, Claude (1986) *The Source of African Philosophy: The Ethiopian Philosophy of Man*. Stuttgart, Steiner

Taddesse Adera and Ali Jimale Ahmed (1995) *Silence Is Not Golden: A Critical Anthology of Ethiopian Literature*. Lawrenceville, Red Sea Press

Ullendorf, Edward (1968) *Ethiopia and the Bible*. London, British Academy

Leocadia

Aguilar, M. and I. Robertson (1984) *Jewish Spain: A Guide*. Madrid, Altalena

Anouilh, Jean (1947) Léocadia. In: *Piecès Roses*. Paris, Calmann-Lévy

Baer, Yitzhak (1992) *A History of the Jews in Christian Spain*, 2nd edn, 2 vols. Philadelphia, The Jewish Publication Society

Beinart, Haim (ed) (1974–1985) *Records of the Trials of the Spanish Inquisition in Cuidad Real*. Jerusalem, The Israel National Academy of Sciences and Humanities

Biale, Rachel (1984) *Women and Jewish Law: An Exploration of Women's Issues in Halakhic Sources*. New York, Schocken

Encyclopaedia Judaica, second edition (2007). Farmington Hills, Thomson Gale

Frances Xavier Cabrini

Barolini H. (ed) (1985) *The Dream Book: An Anthology of Writings by Italian American Women*. New York, Schocken

De Rosa, Tina (1960) *Paper Fish*. New York, Feminist Press

Di Donato, Pietro (1939/1966) *Christ in Concrete*. Indianapolis, Bobbs-Merrill

Gardaphé, Fred L. (1996) *Italian Signs, American Streets: The Evolution of Italian American Narrative*. Durham, Duke University Press

Lentricchia, Frank (1994) *The Edge of Night*. New York, Random House

Torgovnick, Marianna De Marco (1994) *Crossing Ocean Parkway: Readings by an Italian American Daughter*. Chicago, Chicago University Press

Mary

(see also Walata Petros)

Appleyard, David (1993) *Ethiopian Manuscripts*. London, Jed

Chojnacki, Stanislaw (1983) *Major Themes in Ethiopian Paintings: Indigenous Developments, the Influence of Foreign Models and Their Adaptation from the 13th to the 19th Century*. Wiesbaden, Steiner

Cole, Herbert M. (1989) *Icons: Ideals and Power in the Art of Africa*. Washington, Smithsonian Institution

Getatchew Haile (1991) (trans) *The Epistle of Humanity of Emperor Zär'a Ya'aqob*. Scriptorum Christianorum Orientalum 522–523. Leuven, Peeters

Heldman, Marilyn E. (1994) *The Marian Icons of the Painter Fré Seyon: A Study in Fifteenth-Century Ethiopian Art, Patronage, and Spirituality*. Wiesbaden, Harrassowitz

Heldman, Marilyn and Stuart C. Munro-Hay (eds) (1993) *African Zion: The Sacred Art of Ethiopia*. New Haven, Yale University Press

Marcus, Harold G. (1994) *A History of Ethiopia*. Berkeley, University of California Press

Mercier, Jacques (1997) *Art that Heals: The Image as Medicine in Ethiopia*.

New York, Museum of African Art/Prestel

Nooter, Mary H. (1993) *Secrecy: African Art that Conceals and Reveals.* New York, The Museum of African Art

Pollig, Herman (1973) *Religious Art of Ethiopia.* Stuttgart, Insitut für Auslandsbeziehungen

Anne Blonstein was born in England in 1958. Before leaving in 1983, she spent six years in Cambridge, where she took a degree in Natural Sciences followed by a PhD in genetics and plant breeding. She now earns a living as a freelance translator and editor in Basel, Switzerland. The author of four previous poetry books and five chapbooks, she has also collaborated with Swiss composers on several projects.

author photo: Kathrin Schaeppi